Get Up, Girl, Let's Go:
Getting Unstuck and Living Free

ENDORSEMENTS

Are you stuck? Seem to be getting nowhere in your spiritual life? Tracy Hester has some wonderful suggestions to help you step out of failure! You will be brought to a better place as you work through tools that can set you free. While the enemy has destruction in mind, God is for you. Reading this book will give you the heavenly perspective that you need.

—Julie Zine Coleman, author of *On Purpose: Understanding God's Freedom for Women through Scripture* and managing editor of Arise Daily Devotionals

There are times in our life when we either lay down and give up or "girl, get up and try again!" This book is Tracy's story. Her encouraging words and advice are life-giving. We all have things that we feel we will never get over—times when we wonder why God would give us this hard journey. Tracy gives you prompts and sound advice to begin the process of healing and change.

Your past does not define your future. How you begin to change is what counts. This book will begin to take you to places of change. The best people to inspire us are the ones who have gone through the hard knocks of life themselves. You can trust that Tracy is that person. She has listened to God's voice and prompting, done the challenging work, and come out the other side. I will keep this book in my library of references and recommend it to women who need it.

—Phylis Mantelli, author of *Unmothered* and co-author of *She Writes for Him*, Motivational speaker, and Life Coach

Tracy Hester has crafted an anointed work in, *Get Up, Girl, Let's Go*, with boldness, insight, and compassionate love! Her book provides practical applications with scriptural references to guide women and girls from being stuck to new freedom and a more profound faith journey. Tracy's tipping point wisdom can apply to men and boys as well!

—**Janice Edwards**, award-winning, Emmy-nominated talk show host, executive producer, international best-selling co-author, President & CEO of Edwards Unlimited Productions

Get Up, Girl, Let's Go is both an encouraging hug and a gentle kick-in-the-pants prompting us to move forward in God. The book helps us honestly survey our past to understand how it affects our present, so we can gain control and look forward to the abundant future God has in store. In *Get Up, Girl, Let's Go*, Tracy walks with us on this fantastic journey.

—**Dr. Sharon Norris Elliott**, Founder/CEO of AuthorizeMe Consulting, Coaching, & Editing Firm, and Literary Agency LLC

Get Up, Girl, Let's Go is a powerful rallying call to encourage those teetering on the edge of slipping into a pit or seeking a rope of hope to get unstuck from one. If that's you, you're at the brink of your breakthrough! So, grab hold of the lifeline of empowering lessons, Scriptures, resources, and revelation Tracy released through this book to rise. Allow God to heal, restore and renew your strength to run forward into the next best season of your life.

—**Reverend Treva Reid**, East Oakland Council Member

Boldly activate your kingdom-minded potential. Before you read this book, you're going to have to ask yourself, do I want to get unstuck? Am I ready to walk into everything that God has for me? This book is a take up your mat and walk kind of book. Tracy will challenge you to find your complete healing and freedom in Christ and live boldly in who God created you to be. And she brings it with practical meat and potatoes ways to walk it out starting today.

—Amber Weigand-Buckley, multi-award-winning editor and art director of *Leading Hearts* magazine, Owner of #barefacedcreativemedia, Marketing Director for the Advanced Writers and Speakers Association

Get Up, Girl, Let's Go:
Getting Unstuck and Living Free

Tracy Hester

ELK LAKE PUBLISHING INC

PUBLISHING THE POSITIVE
Plymouth, Massachusetts

COPYRIGHT NOTICE

Cover and Interior Design: Amber Weigand-Buckley, Derinda Babcock, Deb Haggerty

Cover Illustration: Ken Weigand

Editor(s): Sue Fairchild, Deb Haggerty

Author Represented By: AuthorizeMe Literary Agency

PUBLISHED BY: Elk Lake Publishing, Inc., 35 Dogwood Drive, Plymouth, MA 02360, 2022

Library Cataloging Data

Names: Hester, Tracy (Tracy Hester)

Get Up, Girl, Let's Go / Tracy Hester]

254 p. 23cm × 15cm (9in × 6 in.)

ISBN-13: 978-1-64949-605-8 (paperback) | 978-1-64949-606-5 (trade paperback) | 978-1-64949-547-1 (e-book)

Key Words: God's presence, intimacy with God, awe, devotional, inspirational, going deeper with God, everyday miracles

Library of Congress Control Number: 2022937579 Nonfiction

DEDICATION

To all the women who desire a deeper intimate relationship with God but feel stuck. May this book inspire you to move past any obstacles or limitations holding you back from experiencing God's perfect love and power in your life.

CONTENTS

ACKNOWLEDGMENTS

Thanks to all the special people who held my hand and encouraged me and at times helped me get up when I didn't think I could:

My parents James and Angelina, my siblings Lori and Reggie, and my extended family. I thank God for the blessing of a loving and supportive family.

To my children CJ and Courtney, the loves of my life and the motivators who remind me I'm not too old to reinvent and transform into Tracy 2.0. Thanks for your patience and unconditional love during the years when I was trying to figure it out.

I want to thank my coach and agent, Sharon, for the endless hours she dedicated to coaching and championing me. Your support has helped a book idea become a resource.

A special thanks to Brenda, my spiritual mentor. You helped inspire me to go deeper in my journey with God as I walked through the most painful season in my life. This journey ignited a passion in me to help hurting women heal and define my God-created purpose.

Thanks to the unique community of women who continue to inspire me to have immense faith to believe in God for the impossible becoming possibilities in my life.

PART ONE: GET UP, GIRL

CHAPTER 1

Unlocking Where the Stuck Started

A few years ago, I visited a museum near my home and became intrigued with an exhibit called the La Brea Tar Pits. My normal museum routine is to look, ooh and aah, and then move on, but with this exhibit I lingered a while to read the history of the Tar Pits. The La Brea Tar Pits is a national historic site located in Los Angeles, California. The pits are filled with this tar, which is natural asphalt that has bubbled up from the ground for the past 10,000–50,000 years.[1] The same type of tar we now use to seal roofs and pave roads had trapped thousands of creatures in these pits. Animals such as mammoths, saber-toothed tigers, wolves, cats, dogs, and bees lost their lives in the sticky, gooey mess.[2]

Why did they get stuck? From a distance, I'm sure the pits looked like a great place to get a cool drink of water, meet with familiar friends, or capture that night's dinner. They had no idea this enticing location was really a trap. Today, the tar pits are fenced in, and animals are protected from getting stuck, but the sticky traps still exist.

Most people have a stuck story or two they can tell. In fact, sticky, gooey, and messy situations seem to be inevitable. Although our stuck stories and the ways we navigate through them are different, we can all relate. Sticky situations can range from being stuck in California traffic to being stuck in a line at the grocery store. Or, better yet, getting stuck in an uncomfortable conversation. Sometimes our sticky situations keep us temporarily stuck, which is okay, because we can see the other side of freedom. Eventually, the traffic and grocery store lines go away, and the painful conversation ends even if we don't like the outcome.

The most influential woman in my life—my mother—has a way of encouraging me to get unstuck. She created motivational quotes designed to inspire me and keep me encouraged, especially when I was having one of my typical moody teenage bad acne days—and those happened often. I knew when my mother was about to start a motivating conversation with me because she would not address me by my name. Instead, she would say, "Guurrlll!" (That's "Girl" with her head leaning forward like a friend about to tell a juicy secret.) She'd then quote one of her famous one-liners:

"Guurrlll, life might get hard, but you need to hang in there."

"Guurrlll, you need to learn how to encourage yourself in the Lord because others will not always encourage you."

"Guurrlll, don't give up, remember you're a tortoise, and slow and steady will win the race."

"Guurrlll, you're not always going to have bad acne! One day you're going to have beautiful skin!"

"Guurrlll, you can stay down for a minute, but you're going to have to get up soon!"

After one of Mommy's lines, I could get up from my emotional pain in the strength of the encouragement given specifically to me—her girl—and move forward because of the inner invitation that spoke, "Let's go," to my heart. Get up, girl, let's go!

We can still find ourselves in stuck situations, however, without encouraging voices to help free ourselves from the pit. That pesky tar follows us home and moves in as an uninvited guest.

Take the example of Denise who I met years ago. To look at her now, one would never guess she had been anything but a moral, educated, "regular" girl. However, she had been stuck for years in the "tar" of drug addiction stemming from the negative, dysfunctional environment in which she had been raised. Her grandfather had sexually molested her when she was only five. She also witnessed her mother's drug abuse and involvement in prostitution— brought on undoubtedly by her depression because of her husband's incarceration. Denise often felt neglected by her family. At the tender age of thirteen, the attention she received from a nineteen-year-old drug dealer proved to be the trigger that shot her into promiscuity and drug abuse.

At age twenty-three, Denise had a son. By the time he turned thirteen, the generational pattern of drug abuse had entered his life too. The negative choices her son made and her arrest for drug abuse became too much for her to handle. Her life started to spin out of control, and she couldn't function any longer. She had hit rock bottom.

She grew tired of the mistakes she was making and finally told herself, "I must do something different or

I'm going to die." Her cry became, "God, please save me. I don't want to do drugs. I don't want to sell my body any more for drugs! If you pull me out of this pit, I'll never go back."

Finally, at the age of thirty-eight, Denise made a life-changing decision and reached out for help.

I know, I know, I hear you. *That worked for Denise. How nice. You don't know my story. This "tar" you speak of has been attached to me for a long time. I don't want anyone to know about my past. Keeping everything to myself is how I'm holding it together.*

I hear you. Because of the "tar" in my life, I felt the same way. Sticky situations tend to make us want to hide. But "tar" isn't just sticky, it stinks too. Like having doggy do on your shoe. You might not know it's there, but everyone around you does. Eventually, you start smelling it too, and you'll do whatever you have to do to get away from that smell. But then you discover it's your shoe that smells and you can't get away until you scrape the dung off and leave that smell behind.

When we're stuck in that sticky, smelly place, we can't see beyond our pit. We can feel our feet sinking, but we don't have the power to pull out. Trying to maneuver ourselves out of our pit is exhausting. We can't grow spiritually and emotionally because our focus is one-dimensional, aimed solely at the present circumstance, dreaming about our escape. Being stuck doesn't allow us to fulfill our greatest potential and become the best versions of ourselves.

Have you ever felt you were not moving forward in your life, but were not sure what was holding you back? You knew something prevented you from growing emotionally and spiritually, but you couldn't put your finger on what. Uncovering what makes us stay stuck is vital because dwelling in a pit only allows us to watch and dream. We can't walk into the plans and purposes God has gifted and called us to be while remaining stuck.

Sometimes our "stuckness" is not as apparent because we have grown accustomed to our pit. This stinky, smelly place has become our new home, our nice and comfortable haven. We start thinking our pit is normal, and we don't see the negative relationship patterns or the invisible chains and fetters holding us securely in our pit.

Negative Relationship Patterns and Invisible Chains and Fetters

In Denise's story we saw the obvious areas where she was stuck—drug and sexual addiction. But Denise's stickiness started when she chose an unhealthy negative relationship.

Negative relationship patterns occur when we repeat the same detrimental behaviors with new people. These patterns can occur in romantic relationships, friendships, and in working relationships. Sometimes our relationship patterns are formulas we use repeatedly without realizing it. Our relationship patterns dictate three things:

1. Who we pick—the people we get into relationships with
2. How we interact—the behaviors we use with those people
3. What we accept—the type of treatment we allow those people to give us

Typical negative relationship patterns include:

1. Trying to change people who do not want to change

2. Demanding control in the relationship—being large and in charge
3. Functioning as the parent in the relationship—being the caretaker, the responsible one
4. Giving up your individuality—functioning totally as the codependent
5. Accepting the instability of a volatile relationship
6. Accepting emotional or physical abuse[3]

You may be able to relate to one or more of these scenarios, or you might be thinking of other patterns in your own life. Can you identify any negative relationship pattern(s) in any area of your life? (Feel free to use any of the six mentioned above.)

What are the triggers causing you to repeat any negative pattern(s)?

Invisible Chains and Fetters

Invisible chains can represent places where we feel trapped in pain, sadness, grief, control, and abuse. Fetters are made of metal and wrapped around the lower leg or foot as a form of imprisonment. A fetter is designed to keep us chained so that our movement is limited. Sounds like cruel and unusual punishment, right? Okay, maybe you haven't experienced being chained, but what about the feeling of being weighed down in a situation? A fetter can also mean anything holding us back or limiting our freedom. For example, we're fettered when we're weighed down by carrying something such as a heavy backpack or by emotionally holding onto a situation that has imprisoned us for years.

It's interesting how we carry things in our purses or backpacks but don't realize how much of a load we're carrying until our shoulders or necks start hurting. Even then, we continue to carry the load and endure the pain because we have an emotional attachment to the things we're carrying. I recently cleaned out my purse and discovered I was carrying too many credit cards—cards from closed accounts and with expired dates. I also had four pairs of glasses—two sunglasses and two reading glasses. Why? The truth is, on the surface, these items might seem excessive to someone else, but the root of why I carried them comes from a deeper need.

My personal story involves negative relationship patterns that caused invisible chains and fetters that kept me stuck for years. I stayed in an unhealthy relationship which led to a divorce after twenty-four years of marriage. Trust me, I did not ever think divorce would be a chapter in my life's story, let alone something I would be writing about in a book. My first lesson about the impact of being stuck happened as I went through the hardships of my marital issues. The divorce hurt me deeply, and for the first time in my life I did not know how to navigate this type of emotional pain. I tried to hide and mask my pain and was slowly drowning. I did not know how to save my marriage or get through the death spiral of a divorce. Would my next steps lead me to the other side of freedom or to a deeper "tar pit"?

At the time, I could not understand why God allowed this to happen to me. I had tried so hard to be a good Christian girl. I was raised in the church. I knew about putting on the armor of God to avoid spiritual attack, and about the enemy's plan to steal, kill, and destroy. However, this was the first time I experienced the enemy personally trying to annihilate me. His mission was to destroy me and my children, convince me I would lose my mind, and cause me to do things that would certainly question my good Christian girl title.

I did not have a manual with ten easy steps on how to survive a divorce and come out healed. Instead, *Tar* became my good friend. Her voice in my head manipulated my perspective about the truth, convinced me to protect my emotions, and played the tape repeatedly about all the bad things I'd ever done to cause my divorce. Tar kept reminding me:

1. What were you thinking when you did that?
2. You don't need community—isolation is a good thing.
3. Don't talk about it—forget about it and it'll go away.
4. Don't tell anyone—they'll judge you.

I listened to Tar. I stayed busy doing things. I enrolled in Bible college and started volunteering my time—all good things to keep me focused externally. But I wasn't focused on the most important thing: the issues of my heart.

Honestly, I didn't know what was going on in my heart. Over the years, I had masterfully learned how to hide my emotions, to not say anything to offend, and to focus on fixing others' issues while my issues stayed hidden away. At times, I felt guilty expressing my feelings and pain. I had become a professional at masking my anger. Thinking it was not of God, I tried to hide my anger from him. I felt disappointed he let this happen to me, but buried the fact I felt he had failed me. I wondered why he was not protecting me. Was God who he says he is? Did he care about me? Was he watching me die in this pain?

I thought I was handling the divorce well until one day my daughter left me a note on the kitchen counter that said, "Mom, I need you to survive!" I instantly broke into tears, and in that moment, I realized I had to stop listening to Tar and get out of my pit. I reached out for help.

Tar has a voice. What is she saying to you?

What Is Your Story?

One of the first things we must uncover on our journey of becoming unstuck is to discover why we're stuck in the first place. What is at the root of our stuckness? I have been asking the Lord for years, "Why are your people not living the victorious and abundant life promised to us in Scripture?" I recently felt I received an answer from him, and it also connects to why he told me to write this book.

God's people are not experiencing the promised land life because of disappointments, residue from our past, and thoughts that don't align with what he says about us. More importantly, trying to unravel the things that have caused us emotional injury is draining!

According to Dr. John Townsend, the author of *Hiding from Love: How to Change the Withdrawal Patterns That Isolate and Imprison You,* "When we experience emotional injury, fear, or shame, our first impulse is to hide the hurting parts of ourselves from God, others, and ourselves. Often, we have learned these hiding patterns during childhood to protect ourselves in threatening environments. The problem is when we hide, we isolate ourselves from the thing we need to heal. What once served as protection as a child can become our prison as an adult."[4]

Stuck in Hiding

We often hide from our pain—our pain from the past, our pain from disappointments, our pain from unfair situations, and our pain from staying silent. Our emotional pain can cause us to become stuck and stay stuck. No one raises their hand and says, "Please give me pain." But when pain is unavoidable, we want our pain to go away quickly. And we think hiding from it will help. Not only do we hide from the memories associated with the pain, but we also hide from the people who caused our pain.

It's not uncommon to withdraw or hide when we are experiencing emotional pain. Some common forms of emotional hiding include shutting down in difficult conversations, stating we're fine when we're not, and putting the people who have caused the emotional injury on time out. Emotional hiding can be a form of protection. We hide our emotions because we fear retaliation, or we don't want to take the risk of discussing a topic that might cause us to relive a negative memory.

Ways You Can Be Stuck

When we are stuck, we are unable to move forward in our life and reach our true potential. So, what's keeping you from achieving your highest potential? Here's a survey to assess specific areas where you might be stuck. Check all that apply.

☐ I feel my circumstances will never change; I've lost hope.

☐ I process more negative thoughts than positive.

☐ I struggle with perfectionism which leads to procrastination; I'm not able to complete the things I want or need to get done.

☐ My life feels like a maze; I'm making little progress in accomplishing my dreams.

☐ I don't know how to communicate effectively in a relationship, so I shut down.

☐ I have secrets I will never tell anyone.

☐ I feel discouraged and confused about my next steps in life.

☐ I often wonder what my purpose is.

☐ I feel uncomfortable with establishing healthy boundaries in relationships for the fear of confrontation or rejection.

☐ I hide my true feelings to avoid judgment.

☐ I criticize myself and others openly or secretly.

☐ I have trust issues with others.

☐ I spend too much time in my head telling myself what I haven't done.

☐ I'm afraid to take risks.

☐ I compare myself to other women.

☐ I feel guilt and shame from a mistake(s).

☐ I keep making the same misjudgments in romantic relationships.

☐ My identity is based upon my performance; I don't know who I am outside of my role or title.

☐ I think I'll never be able to forgive what happened to me.

☐ I work harder to suppress my feelings of disappointment in the areas where I feel a void.

☐ I don't fit in or feel qualified sometimes.

Please don't feel you've flunked if you checked a lot or passed if you only checked a few. This is not a test and there is no passing or failing grade. Everyone gets 100 percent for completing this exercise because you have completed the first step in getting unstuck— recognizing something is off balance in your life.

How do you feel about identifying potential stuck areas in your life?

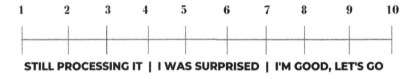

STILL PROCESSING IT | I WAS SURPRISED | I'M GOOD, LET'S GO

Possibly, you have been stuck in a pit for as long as you can remember, and you can't see yourself being set free. You've accepted being stuck as the only option available—it might even be comfortable. Well, I have good news for you. These pits are not permanent! You don't have to live in them forever. Becoming aware and being truthful with yourself and with God about the areas blocking you from experiencing your best life is where the transformation of getting unstuck starts.

Do you want to know the solution to breaking free from that stuck place and finding a solid foundation on which to stand? The solution and solid foundation are in Jesus Christ. Psalm 40:1–3 promises, "I waited patiently for the LORD to help me, and he turned to me and heard my cry. He lifted me out of the pit of despair, out of the mud and the mire. He set my feet on solid ground and steadied me as I walked along. He has given me a new song to sing, a hymn of praise to our God. Many will see what he has done and be amazed. They will put their trust in the LORD."

We have a biblical example of Jesus going out of his way to pull a woman out of her pit. In John 4:2–26, we read the account of a Samaritan woman, also known as the woman at the well. This woman was in a deep cycle of guilt and shame that held her hostage in her pit. She also had invisible chains and fetters pulling her down deeper into her pit. Her story included a pattern of sexual promiscuity, guilt, shame, and a fractured self-esteem, all causing her to repeat negative relationship patterns with men. She had sunk low. So low she decided to draw water from a well during the hottest part of the day, a time when no one else would be there. She didn't want to interact with anyone who might judge her or remind her she was not accepted or good enough. She didn't see a way out of her sin and daunting circumstances until she met someone who changed her life. That someone was Jesus.

Can you identify with this woman? Have you made some questionable choices in your life? Have those choices mired you in a pit of guilt, shame, and despair? Do you go out of your way to avoid people because of this? Are you tired of being stuck in a pit? Is the load you're carrying too heavy? Are you ready to start unpacking the weight?

We need to dig further to free ourselves from our pit. What holds you back or keeps you from moving on?

Now that you've identified some of the things holding you in that tar pit, you might feel a little overwhelmed. The journey ahead might challenge your thinking at times, but I want to encourage you to stick with the process. I promise if you complete this journey, you will grow spiritually and emotionally.

To help you along your journey, every chapter will end with a section encouraging you to Get Up, Girl, Let's Go!

GET UP: Based on the topics discussed in each chapter, these sections challenge you to think about yourself—where might you need healing, how you can adopt new ways of thinking, or what inspires you.

GIRL: These sections contain encouraging and loving voices from yourself and others to motivate and cheer you on.

LET'S GO: These sections will engage your spiritual self, reminding you God is with you always. He is intricately concerned about your success. He wants to help you get and remain unstuck and to become the God-created version he intended.

Let's get started on the first Get Up, Girl, Let's Go exercise. As a reminder there are three prompts in this exercise:

Get Up, Girl, Let's Go Exercise:

Review the specific stuck areas you've checked on pages 11-12 and then list the five you identify with the most.

1.

2.

3.

4.

5.

Create your own Get Up, Girl, Let's Go motivational quote—something to encourage and inspire you on your journey. For example: "I'm stuck right now, but this is only temporary. Soon I will get unstuck and watch who I become!"

My Get Up, Girl motivational quote:

Think about God saying this to you: "Now that you've identified areas in your life where you are stuck, I want to remind you I am with you as you take one step at a time on this journey. I'm holding your hand on this journey as we leap over the bumps and potholes to get to the other side. I'm leading you, not pulling you, but only walking ahead of you because I can see what you can't see. I will make all your crooked paths straight. Will you have an open mind and trust me the entire way? I will never leave you or reject you. I love you."

Proverbs 3:5–6 says, "Trust in the Lord with all your heart; do not depend on your own understanding. Seek his will in all you do, and he will show you which path to take."

Reflection:

What resonates with you after you read this Scripture? What is the promise God offers if you trust him and seek his will in your life?

CHAPTER 2

Creating Your Life Map

A life map is a tool designed to help you move forward toward a new destination, to help you get unstuck. The life map's purpose is to bring you clarity on how you've ended up where you are, and how previous experiences, events, and people have shaped your belief system, values, and self-worth. The key is to uncover how specific patterns and choices have taken you off course and how others have played a role in guiding or distracting you from your purpose and destiny.[1]

Mapping your past to get a deeper understanding of how you arrived where you are allows you to revisit parts of your life you didn't realize were so significant. All the experiences, events, and people in your past have worked together to lead you down the path you are now on.

Creating a life map of your story will also lead you to a place of deeper clarity and self-awareness. When you spend concentrated time looking at your life, it's hard to ignore the roadblocks, tar, and pits that present themselves. You will have a few "aha" moments and might say, "How did I not know this about myself?" By looking back, you might find yourself reconnecting with a part of yourself you left behind. Let's get started.

My Life Map —Use the journal on the next page to elaborate on each of the 10 events.

start

AGE _____

EVENT 1. _____

AGE _____

EVENT 2. _____

AGE _____

EVENT 3. _____

_____

AGE _____

EVENT 4. _____

AGE _____

EVENT 5. _____

_____

AGE _____

EVENT 6. _____

AGE _____

EVENT 7. _____

AGE _____

EVENT 8. _____

_____

AGE _____

EVENT 9. _____

AGE _____

EVENT 10. _____

_____

Life Map Journal — Journal below and elaborate on each of the 10 events from your Life Map.

1. _____

_____

2. _____

_____

3. _____

_____

4. _____

_____

5. _____

_____

6. _____

_____

7. _____

_____

8. _____

_____

9. _____

_____

10. _____

_____

Creating Your Life Map

Step One:

On your life map journal, write ten important events representing your life. Important doesn't have to be exciting or memorable as defined by others. This map depicts what is important to you. Events you might consider as important are:

- Events that have taught you something about life such as the value of family, working hard, perseverance.
- Events shifting the direction of your life.
- Events that made you feel special or sad.
- Events that have made you who you are today—career, marriage, kids, ministry.
- Events highlighting how vital life is to you.

Step Two:

- Look at your map from start to finish or as a timeline. Start from childhood and go to where you are now.
- Transfer your important events onto your life map. Title your event and include your age at the time of the event. Be sure to list events chronologically.

Step Three:

The characters on the life map template are for illustrative purposes only and not to guide you on what events you should include on your map. Add additional labels, pictures, or symbols to your map—feel free to be creative.

Step Four:

Review your life map and answer the following questions.

Where did you start your map? Which event is first?

Where have you been? Evaluate your past.

Where are you now?

Did any event shift the trajectory of your life?

What were the seasons in which God protected you?

Were there any seasons when you walked in sin?

Were there any times you felt alone or fearful?

Identify what specific event(s) contributed to you being stuck. Why did you become stuck?

Who caused you to get stuck? i.e., me, siblings, parents, friends, a person in a relationship.

Keep your life map handy; we'll reference it in future chapters.

Jeremiah 29:11 is one of my favorite verses because it brings us so much hope when we feel stuck. "'For I know the plans I have for you,' says the LORD, 'They are plans for good and not for disaster, to give you a future and a hope." In this verse, the prophet Jeremiah affirms that God is in control, and he has good things for us. Based upon this Scripture, what does God have for you?

1. God has _____ for me.

2. God's plans are to_____me not to _____me.

3. God's plans are to give me _____and a_____.

The Bible is full of examples of people going through trying times and learning lessons that mature them and help them see their life as God sees it. I know feeling fearful, sad, rejected, and abandoned is not what you want, nor is it the plan God has for you. His plans for you are to prosper you and not to harm you. His plans give hope and a bright future. Take a moment and process God's plans for you.

It's important to realize God is for you and not against you. Although you may have experienced difficulties in your past, and these may be the reasons you are stuck currently, I have good news for you! Jesus Christ is your champion. He wants to come alongside you right in your situations to lift you out of the pit that's been immobilizing you for years. He is the one who is coming to answer your prayers. He is reminding you to be still and let him do the heavy lifting because his load is easy, and his burden is light. Will you take Jesus's hand and allow him to take you on a journey called freedom?

Get Up, Girl, Let's Go Exercise:

What dream(s) have you not been able to fulfill because of an event on your life map?

What wisdom would you give the younger version of yourself? What encouragement can you speak over your mistakes and choices?

Think about God saying this to you: "You have questioned, 'Why did this happen to me?' and thought, *This is sooooo unfair.* But be encouraged, because I take you through seasons of contradictions for a reason, and I can turn your contradictions into beautiful gifts if you allow me. I know the contradictions in your life make you pause and shake your head and say, 'Why? Why did that happen to me, God? Why am I being falsely accused? Why did my child have to die? Why am I fighting cancer? And why did the relationship end? God, why am I stuck?'

"Sometimes, contradictions don't make sense, especially when you feel you've done everything right, and the punishment you're experiencing doesn't fit the crime. I've heard your prayers. I've seen how you have trusted me when you couldn't see beyond being stuck. You have done everything your human mind can conjure. I am God, and I have a plan to use your contradictions to teach and mature you spiritually. I want you to learn who I am. I am your Father, and I love you. Daughter, I desire for you to learn how to be in a relationship with me. The deeper you go in learning about and experiencing me, the more you will discover who I am and who you are. I've pushed you out of your comfort zone to mature you into the woman I have called you to be. The God-created version of you. From a place of contradiction, I want you to decide to put in the work to mature spiritually. I want you to not remain stuck.

"What should you do when you feel stuck? Continue to trust me and allow me to lead you through a process to get you unstuck. If you allow me to do the work of healing you, the gift that comes forth will be a courageous, fearless woman who is not afraid to face her stuck areas head-on because she has learned to trust in me."

"We can rejoice, too, when we run into problems and trials, for we know that they will help us develop strength of character, and character strengthens our confident hope of salvation" (Romans 5:3–4).

Reflection:

How do you desire to grow in your spiritual walk?

CHAPTER 3

Facing Your Past

Congratulations on completing your life map. You might be feeling a little overwhelmed by it all. Did thinking about your childhood bring up any sad memories or anger? Maybe you were surprised about a cycle (or cycles) you have been repeating for years. Possibly you noticed a negative relationship pattern or two, or realized you had been suppressing a memory for many years. You might be shaking your head and thinking, "Wow, I've been through more than I thought." Likewise, I'm sure you've also noticed positive patterns and cycles on your map, and those memories made you smile and laugh.

What have you learned about yourself from looking at your life map? Did anything surprise you?

I learned:

I was surprised about:

In this chapter, we'll focus on facing the negative parts of our past and explore a different perspective. Everyone is at a different stage in their healing process. You might feel as if you are not healing at all, or you might feel healed but have some leftover residue. I want to encourage you. Your individual healing journey is a process, and it can take some time. The goal is to start the process. However, the healing process cannot begin until we face it.

Where are you in your process?

TOTALLY STUCK | WORKING ON IT | I'VE DEALT WITH IT

Circle the emoji(s) you feel when you think about your past.

List two events from your past that make you smile.

1.

2.

List two events from your past you don't care to talk about.

1.

2.

The first time I completed a life map, I immediately noticed a recurring pattern from my past—an ugly cycle of rejection. My earliest memory of when the rejection started was from fourth grade. I vividly remember not being chosen and accepted by my classmates. At recess time, we would play kickball. I wasn't as good as some of the other kids, but my competitive spirit had one goal—to kick the ball over the playground fence like some of the other good players.

There was only one problem. None of the kids wanted me on their team. So, sometimes I would be chosen last or not at all. The only exception was when my older brother was a team captain. He would pick me first because he didn't want me to feel left out.

I didn't like the feeling of not being chosen so I worked hard over the summer to improve my kickball skills. My hard work paid off. During a game on my brother's team the next school year, I kicked the ball over the fence! Now the other kids started picking me to be on their teams. I learned working hard to be the best and excelling above and beyond was required to be chosen and accepted.

I also remembered a time when I didn't make my high school cheerleading squad. The reason? I was better at basketball than cheerleading. I cried for days after not making the cheer team. A week later, one of the girls dropped out, and I was asked to join as her replacement. I gladly accepted and felt overjoyed. I remember thinking, "I'm now good enough to be a cheerleader." Again, the need to prove my worth made me work hard at becoming skilled at cheering. I wanted to show why I should have been their first choice. Being accepted on the squad reinforced that hard work would get me what I needed: approval and acceptance by others.

Having a solid work ethic became part of my character, but so did my fear of being rejected—not being good enough to be chosen first. Why did my hard work only garner me a second-place trophy? I worked hard to be successful professionally, and whatever I committed to do, I did with excellence.

When it came to having a successful romantic relationship, however, I seemed to fail consistently. I often chose men who were not able to connect at a deeper emotional level. As a result, they would not put me in first place in their lives. The consequences of my bad choices cost me years of pain, therapy, and low self-esteem.

Repeated rejection convinced me I was defective, unredeemable, and unlovable. It also wired me to become a performance driven person—a pattern I continued throughout college and when I started dating my future husband.

Would you be surprised to hear I was not my ex-husband's first choice? When I met him at a party, he was interested in someone else, but she wasn't interested in him. Once again, I came in second. But at least, I had still been chosen. I didn't realize being the second-choice pick would not serve me well. I worked hard to become a first-choice option, but was unsuccessful.

God used the life map exercise to open my eyes to the deeper side of the patterns of rejection operating in me. I honestly wasn't aware of how the enemy tried to destroy my life starting at the age of ten, and how this cycle continued for over forty years.

Honoring Your Past

Our lives are sometimes like a movie. Some scenes have action, other scenes make us cry, and some scenes cause us to shout for joy. There are high drama segments, romantic moments, and scary parts. Though a movie can be written to be funny, scary, or sad, the film can impact each viewer differently. In the same way, a situation that traumatizes one person might roll off another person's back with little effect at all. How situations affect us is all a matter of perspective.

Our perspective is how we look at life. Like a camera with a panoramic view, when we look through the lens, we see a wide view from the left to the right. Our perspective influences our attitudes, mindsets, opinions, beliefs, and outlook on life. Events in our childhood—both positive and negative—shape our perspective and determine our opinions about life.

Honoring Your Past with a New Perspective

A change of perspective means there is a change in our attitude about something, and a shift in how we think. We can't change our past or resolve a problem by complaining, but we can solve and learn to accept our past or the problem by approaching it from a new perspective. A pessimist might see their past as negative. An optimist might see their past as an opportunity and a possibility for growth. We can honor our past by reframing problems into opportunities.

Would you consider yourself more of an optimist or more of a pessimist when you think about your past? Explain why?

I'll never forget the season of torment I went through when I searched for ways to heal from the pain of my divorce. I had this negative recording repeatedly playing in my head about what happened. A 24/7 reminder of the events leading to the divorce, what transpired during the divorce, what was said, the accusations, and the many questions and fears about my future. How was I supposed to forgive and move away from my past when my past wouldn't go away?

The trauma and drama of the negative memories stuck to me. My mind kept making up scenarios for closure, but, of course, they were all negative. I needed help to process it all, forget about my past, and move on to my all-things-new life.

My perspective about my divorce changed when a good friend from church invited me and other ladies to her home for an overnight sleepover. As we fellowshipped and laughed together, our time turned into a prayer session. My friend began to pray over each of us. I welcomed the prayer, but also knew my friend was prophetic. I wondered what God would tell her about me. When it was my time to sit in the prayer hot seat, she told me what she saw.

A thick snake wrapped around my neck trying to suffocate and kill me.

Honestly, I wasn't taken aback by the picture of the snake. What she saw resonated with me.

Satan accuses us before God day and night; it's his full-time job. Revelation 12:10 says, "Then I heard a loud voice shouting across the heavens, 'It has come at last—salvation and power and the Kingdom of our God, and the authority of his Christ. For the accuser of our brothers and sisters has been thrown down to earth—the one who accuses them before our God day and night.'"

A good friend always reminds me that Satan needs our help to destroy us. My murder would happen with my own self-defeating words, negative thoughts, negative confessions, and belief in the lies Satan told me. The more eye-opening part for me was I agreed with what the enemy said about me instead of trusting what God spoke about me in Scripture.

The prayer session was the catalyst to turn on a light in me. When I discovered the enemy was trying to destroy me, I became more alert and sober-minded than before. I started to see how the enemy had been setting me up since childhood, and I had been trying to figure out my own strategy for healing.

But after this prayer session, a new courage to fight back and save myself emerged. Until this moment, I hadn't understood the meaning of surrendering to God's love. I consider that experience the day I died to myself. Yes, the transition happened suddenly. I knew without a shadow of doubt God had come to help me change my perspective.

The enemy has a plan for our life—to steal, kill, and destroy us. The enemy doesn't want us to experience the abundant and victorious life promised to us in Scripture. He doesn't want us to live a life filled with joy, which is experienced when we're in a relationship with God. His destructive plans are accomplished by setting us up in situations which cause us to doubt God. He wants us to feel insecure and to operate in fear instead of faith. Doubt, fear, and insecurity—all keep us stuck in our pits.

First Peter 5:8 remind us to "Stay alert! Watch out for your great enemy, the devil. He prowls around like a roaring lion, looking for someone to devour."

God wants us to be alert. In other words, we must recognize when the enemy is accusing us.

The Power of Shifting Our Perspective

In her book, *Lies Women Believe: And the Truth That Sets Them Free,* Nancy Leigh DeMoss focuses on the lies we believe about our past and circumstances.[1] After reading the book, I was challenged with this question, "Am I experiencing unnecessary disappointment, pain, anger, and suffering because the enemy is tricking me to believe a lie about me?"

Here are five lies we can believe about our past or present circumstances. Read the lie. Recite the Scripture to counteract the lie and write a new perspective declaration:

Lie	Scripture	New Perspective Declaration
If my circumstances were different, I would be different.	2 Corinthians 5:17: "This mean that anyone who belongs to Christ has become a new person. The old life is gone; a new life has begun!"	
I shouldn't have to suffer. I deserve better.	James 1:2–4: "Dear brothers and sisters, when troubles of any kind come your way, consider it an opportunity for great joy. For you know that when your faith is tested, your endurance has a chance to grow. So let it grow, for when your endurance is fully developed, you will be perfect and complete, needing nothing."	

My circumstances will never change.	1 Corinthians 10:13: "The temptations in your life are no different from what others experience. And God is faithful. He will not allow the temptation to be more than you can stand. When you are tempted, he will show you a way out so that you can endure."	
I'm about to lose my mind. I can't take it anymore.	Isaiah 26:3: "You will keep in perfect peace all who trust in you, all whose thoughts are fixed on you!"	
What about me? It's my turn. She/He hurt me. You don't know what I've been through.	Ephesians 4:31–32: "Get rid of all bitterness, rage, anger, harsh words, and slander, as well as all types of evil behavior. Instead, be kind to each other, tenderhearted, forgiving one another, just as God through Christ has forgiven you."	

The Possibilities of God's Perspective

Scientists estimate the human eye can only see three miles. Contrast that with God's perspective. Isaiah 46:10 says, "Only I can tell you the future before it even happens. Everything I plan will come to pass, for I do whatever I wish." Although our vision is limited,

God can see our beginning and our end. Everything we go through has a purpose.

Romans 8:28 says, "And we know that God causes everything to work together for the good of those who love God and are called according to his purpose for them." Not only can God see our beginning and our end, but he has watched over all the things we have experienced in our lives—the good, the bad, and the ugly are working together to create something good in us.

Although we can't see what is in our future, God sees our future clearly. He is using our circumstances and difficulties to stitch together our beautiful story, one stitch at a time. He uses our most difficult times to conform us to his image and to shift us into our God-created purpose—what he has created us to be.

During the most challenging time in my life, I discovered my purpose. I didn't recognize it at the time, but God was setting me up for a wild ride, the healing journey of a lifetime. He was also opening doors for me to step into my God-created purpose. He used the divorce to start my healing and the process of discovering my purpose.

To be honest, I don't think I would have been compelled or drawn to think about my kingdom purpose without going through pain. God knows me well. I'm a creature of habit who wants my life to be predictable and stable. The divorce threw me off track for a moment, but then God's grace came along, and he used the pain to push me into my purpose.

We can form a new perspective about our past based upon God's grace as the foundation of who we are, instead of our past defining our identity. God's perspective always offers us grace, love, hope, and unconditional acceptance. Grace is defined as the love and mercy given to us by God. It is a gift from God—we don't have to perform perfectly to earn grace, it's free. I think of God's grace as his favor and help when we make a mess of things and when we don't deserve it.

When God's grace steps into our circumstances, things start shifting, closed doors start opening, healing starts happening, and light starts shining in us, allowing us to view our life from God's perspective. The Bible says God's grace is sufficient. In other words, God's grace is unlimited power given to us to do what we could never do on our own. It's sufficient, so it's everything we need.

So, how do we obtain grace? By asking God for it. One way we can show grace to ourselves and others is by letting things go. What a beautiful gift to give ourselves and others.

Proverbs 18:21 puts it this way, "The tongue can bring death or life; those who love to talk will reap the consequences." Our words can speak life or death, and our tongues can build up or tear down.

Let's practice applying grace over our past by declaring a new storyline. We can build ourselves up by the words we speak. The goal is to speak God's perspective over our circumstances. Here are four declarations based upon God's perspective we can adopt:

Declaration #1: What happened in my life was not a mistake.

Since what happened in my life was not a mistake, I am not a mistake. My life story includes many chapters, both good and not so good, but it is still my story. I will come into agreement with what happened. I will no longer remain stuck on the chapters that made me cry and caused pain in my life.

What new positive perspective can you create about your past? Reframe it into a new positive story.

Declaration # 2: I will look at my life from a heavenly perspective.

I choose to look at my life from a heavenly perspective. God allowed certain things to happen in my life for a reason. I come into agreement with Romans 8:28 which says, "And we know that God causes everything to work together for the good of those who love God and are called according to his purpose for them." I understand what happened might not have been good, but God has used it for good.

Can you think of two positive things produced from your past?

Declaration # 3: My past is over. I will focus on my future.

My past does not define my future. God, I give you any negative memory of my past not serving my best interest. God, I give you all memories blocking me from seeing how you see me. You see me as fearfully and wonderfully made. God, I am chosen and lavishly loved by you. Please remove all shame, guilt, unforgiveness, anger, doubt, or unbelief attached to me because of my past. I look forward to the new things you have promised to me in Scripture. I decree and declare my future is determined by God. Philippians 3:13–15 (TPT) says, "I don't depend on my own strength to accomplish this; however I do have one compelling focus: I forget all of the past as I fasten my heart to the future instead. I run straight for the divine invitation of reaching the heavenly goal and gaining the victory-prize through the anointing of Jesus. So let all who are fully mature have this same passion, and if anyone is not yet gripped by these desires, God will reveal it to them."

List and describe three things you can do in your life now to make your future life happen the way you desire?

Declaration # 4: I will no longer keep secrets from God.

I make a covenant to no longer hide from God. I take off my Superwoman cape and come clean about every detail of my life. Including the ones I've hidden and don't want to talk about. Also, the memories resurfacing as I've been reading this book. Today, I declare, I will have no more secrets with God! God, I know you are ready and willing to help me when I am ready and willing to surrender. You are the original counselor who created me, and you know exactly what I need. When I ask you for what I need, you listen. Thank you.

Matthew 7:7–11 says, "Keep on asking, and you will receive what you ask for. Keep on seeking, and you will find. Keep on knocking, and the door will be opened to you. For everyone who asks, receives. Everyone who seeks, finds. And to everyone who knocks, the door will be opened. You parents—if your children ask for a loaf of bread, do you give them a stone instead? Or if they ask for a fish, do you give them a snake? Of course not! So if you sinful people know how to give good gifts to your children, how much more will your heavenly Father give good gifts to those who ask him."

Releasing Our Past

Moses mastered the art of having a face-to-face, open, and honest conversation with God. In Exodus 33, God tells Moses to take the people he had brought out of Egypt to Canaan, the promised land. In other words, Moses was to lead the people to their freedom. This was exciting news, but there was one big problem. God also told Moses he would not be going with them this time.

God refused to accompany the sinful Israelites on their journey to Canaan, lest he be compelled to destroy them on the way because of their arrogant and stubborn behavior. Instead, he would send an angel as his representative. In the wilderness, God had provided for their every need. Instead of being thankful, they complained. The eleven-day trip into the promised land turned into a forty-year journey because of their murmuring and complaining. The Israelites didn't trust God's way. They wanted to do things their way.

Moses knew there was no possible way he could take the Israelites into the Canaan without God. So, Moses decided he would share his heart and concerns with God. Moses asked for God's presence to lead his people to Canaan. The angel representative would not suffice.

The conversation Moses had with God changed God's mind. As a result, God promised his presence would go with them to Canaan. What did Moses say and do that had such a powerful effect on God? Let's break down their conversation as noted in Exodus 33:11–17 to get a better understanding.

- Verse 11: Moses and God were friends. Having a face-to-face with God meant Moses had an open and honest conversation with him.

- Verse 12: God knew Moses, and Moses had found favor with God. Moses had opened his heart to allow God in. Moses was vulnerable with God about his strengths, weaknesses, and failures. God knew Moses's heart.

- Verse 13: Moses craved more of God and prayed for the Israelites. Moses desired to learn God's ways so he would know him better. Moses wasn't satisfied with their relationship. Moses experienced many unique encounters with God, such as the opening of the Red Sea, the burning bush incident, and his abundant provision while the Israelites wandered in the wilderness. Still, Moses craved a fresh encounter with God. God satisfies those who hunger for him (see Matthew 5:6). Moses also reminded God that the Israelites were his people.

- Verse 14: God reversed his previous threat and agreed that his presence would accompany them into Canaan.

- Verse 15–16: Moses reiterated to God how serious he was about God's presence going with them. He knew they would not be able to thrive without God's presence. Moses exposed his heart to God and said to him again, "If you don't personally go with us, don't make us leave this place." Moses understood God's presence was essential. In essence, Moses was saying, "God, if you don't go, we don't go." He would rather stay in the desert with God than go into the promised land without him.

- Verse 17: God was pleased with Moses and told him, "I will indeed do what you have asked, for I look favorably on you, and I know you by name."

In summary, we can glean a couple of things from God and Moses's conversation. First, Moses and God had a great friendship. Second, Moses felt comfortable having an open and honest conversation with God. Moses was raw with God, and God honored Moses's transparency. God responded to his friend, Moses, by listening and acting swiftly to answer his request. God knew Moses's heart and, because his heart was upright, he found favor in his sight. God is our friend. We can have a face-to-face open and honest conversation with him about anything, including our past.

Get Up, Girl, Let's Go Exercise:

As with Moses, God desires our friendship too. Don't be shy about having face-to-face, open, and honest conversations with God. Tell him about your fear, anxiety, guilt, shame, disappointment, and anything else on your heart. God's will is for you to be healed and set free from any and everything keeping you separated from receiving true freedom in your life. Write a letter to God and tell him exactly what's on your heart.

Talk to God as if he was your friend. Listen to how he might respond. What did you hear him say?

"And you will know the truth, and the truth will set you free" (John 8:32).

There is a difference between what is true and the truth. What is true can change because it can be subjective, but the truth never changes. We often believe our experiences, people's opinions, a diagnosis, or what we feel is the truth. God taught me what I thought was true was often a lie. I was diagnosed with sciatica, pain in the lower back caused by irritation of the sciatic nerve. I went to physical therapy, but I wasn't getting better, and my condition seemed to worsen. I decided my lack of progress was because I wasn't following my homecare exercises, so I picked up the pace, but the pain still didn't improve. I decided to stop physical therapy. I didn't see any results, so why continue? I didn't want to go back to my doctor because I was convinced something else might be wrong. I was afraid to find out the truth. Instead, I learned to manage my pain. Sciatica became my new best friend. I talked about her all the time. I made allowances for her. I stopped wearing high heels because it might irritate her. It was her fault I couldn't run, stand for an extended period, bend, or exercise. Sciatica was getting on my *nerves* and making my life miserable.

One day, I ran into a friend who is a personal trainer. She talked me into doing sessions with her. Of course, I had to tell her about Sciatica to see if she could work with both of us. She agreed we would start slow, and my exercise program would be tailored to strengthen both of us. After a few weeks of training, she noticed my hips were weak, especially on my right side.

"You need to go back to your doctor because there might be something else going on," she said.

Of course, I didn't want to hear that, but I already thought the same thing. Reluctantly, I made an appointment with my doctor, and I was told I needed to go back to physical therapy. This time, I asked to be referred to a different rehab center.

At the end of my first session, the physical therapist said, "I don't think you have sciatica. My guess is you have a mild form of arthritis in your hips which is causing your pain."

I said, "What? No way."

But after three months of working with my new therapist and my trainer on exercises to improve my hips—not my back—my condition improved by 90 percent. The lessons God taught me through this experience were:

1. Stop self-diagnosing: If you want to heal, you need to treat what's going on and not what you think is the best treatment. No more self-diagnosing.

2. Seek the truth: God used two people to lead me into the truth and that resulted in my healing. God can use anybody or anything to turn a situation or diagnosis around.

3. Don't be afraid: I suffered longer than necessary because I was afraid of what the truth might reveal—more pain (a lie). The truth would set me free.

4. Remember God's grace and mercy: God answers prayer. In January, I wrote in my journal I wanted to be healed from sciatica. In November, I was healed from arthritis. Despite my ignorance regarding the correct diagnosis, God remained faithful in leading me into his truth. Fear can paralyze—it brings punishment, hopelessness, worry, and insecurity. The solution for fear is to walk in God's love, which is the truth, and never changes. We don't have to be afraid when God gives us the ability and power to be set free.

Reflection:

Are you afraid to face something? If yes, what would be the consequences if you continue to be afraid in this area? What would be the consequences if you faced your fears in this area? What is one way you can apply God's truth to overshadow this fear?

CHAPTER 4

Surrendering Your Broken Parts

I asked a few of my friends what they thought of when they heard the word "surrender." More specifically, I wanted to know how the word made them feel. Did they consider surrender to be more positive or negative? I was not surprised by their responses.

They perceived surrender to be more negative than positive, and I would have to agree. When I asked myself the same question, a picture rose in my mind of someone getting arrested—handcuffed and read their Miranda Rights. I saw this person as basically surrendering to the police.

As I thought more about the picture of someone getting arrested, I wondered about my negative mindset. Did it stem from all the arrests I've been watching on the news lately? Or was it because, at the core of me, I do not want to give up my free will to anyone?

What are your thoughts about the word surrender? How does the word make you feel? What previous experiences might influence your mindset around surrendering?

The *Oxford English Dictionary*'s definition of the word surrender is "cease resistance to an enemy or opponent and to submit to their authority."[1] *Merriam-Webster* says surrendering involves giving up completely or agreeing to forgo especially in favor of another.[2]

The spiritual definition of the word surrender is different from the dictionary's definition. In our Christian vocabulary, we use the word surrender often. For example, there is a famous hymn entitled "I Surrender All" and another entitled "We Surrender It All to You." I have heard pastors and spiritual leaders say the word *surrender* in their sermons. They say things like, "You need to surrender it to God," or "Living a life for God requires us to surrender daily."

To spiritually surrender means a believer ultimately gives up his own will, and subjects his thoughts, ideas, and deeds to the will of God and teachings in the Bible. Unlike the dictionary's definition, there are two key differences about surrender for a Christian. On the one hand, we surrender to a single authority—God—not just any other person of dominion or authority. On the other hand, in spiritual surrender, it's important to note the God to whom we are surrendering is not an enemy or opponent.

Surrendering one's will to God is not easy. For me, the surrender process challenged me for several reasons.

First, I did not understand the process of surrendering to God. Second, I had no clue what I needed to surrender. And third, I perceived surrendering as a huge disadvantage, not something that would benefit me.

The Process of Surrendering to God

Surrendering always requires giving something up. When we surrender to God, however, we don't give up in the way we usually define conceding. It does not mean we stop trying to do something or we abort or abandon our mission in life. Instead, surrendering to God means we stop trying to improve the condition of our issues and the direction of our lives on our own. We yield and concede to God's way of working things out without trying to force our own solutions. We don't give up on the situation, but we give up on the notion we should control or manage it. Instead, we give—surrender—the navigation and control of our lives to God.

What desires do you have in your life that feel difficult to surrender to God? Is there a situation in your life you are currently trying to control? Journal about it below.

The Need to Surrender Control

Initially, the concept of surrendering to God's authority was not an issue for me. I had surrendered to God by giving him my heart. I often surrendered my will by being obedient to following God's Word. I was also living the life of a good Christian woman, wife, mother, and friend. In my mind, I was doing the surrendering thing right.

Despite all my surrendering, though, my life was still unraveling at a speed I could not control. I did not realize I had not truly surrendered everything. As I watched the unraveling of my marriage, I worked harder and harder to fix it myself. I would save my marriage by praying and fasting. I would bind that devil up myself and release him from my life. But all my hard work didn't change anything. In fact, the more spiritual I thought I became because of my "holy" actions, the worse the situation became. One thing was clear—this pending divorce situation was above my pay grade. I would not be able to control or fix anything about it.

I discovered giving up my will, desires, thoughts, responses, plans, and control to God in this situation would not be easy at all. Either I would continue to keep trying to fix everything (and probably keep failing and mentally derail), or I would take my hands completely off the wheel and surrender to whatever God decided to do.

God always offers us a way through and out of our negative circumstances by way of the surrendering process. In my opinion, we have three surrender choices: self-initiated, God-initiated, or no thank you.

If we choose no thank you, we're in for the bumpiest ride. When we refuse to listen to God's word about our situation, we keep self-destructing.

Conversely, when the surrendering is God-initiated, it's typically because he wants to get our attention. He does so by shifting and taking things away without asking. Our response to him taking control might look like a temper tantrum. When we're not ready to give God complete control, we go kicking and screaming. Perhaps we decide he can control 80 percent, but the remaining 20 percent is off limits. If God initiates the surrender, and we still insist on doing things our way, he will intensify our bumpy ride. Then, when we have been adequately humbled, and we are ready to say, "Okay, God you take the wheel from here," God steps in and takes complete control of the navigation of our life.

Or we can self-initiate our surrender. In this position, we go to God and tell him we're giving him the steering wheel of our lives—that includes our checkbooks, our calendars, and our relationships. We're happy to give it all to him, and thankful the load and burden is lifted off our shoulders.

What areas of your life do you feel you are unable to surrender completely to God? What percentage of your life have you given to God and what percentage are you holding on to? Why?

Surrendering My Flaws

Sometimes, you can't tell something is broken because it still works even if it's flawed. When we're dealing with our flaws, we sometimes would rather hide them than own them.

I remember an incident when I was in the ninth grade. My mother bought me a pair of Famolare High Wave Platform shoes. They were the shoes to have back in the '70s. They were an all-leather shoe with a three and one-half-inch rollercoaster wedge. Mine were dark blue. I valued my shoes because they were fashionable and expensive.

The school year had just started. One day, I ripped the top part of my left shoe on a nail. My heart sank. I showed my mother what happened, and she said, "We can take it to the shoe repair shop, and they can fix it and make it good as new." They did fix my shoe, but it did not look as good as new. Anyone could see my shoe was now flawed and no longer perfect. My beautiful new shoes were ruined, and I was embarrassed to wear them. I had one problem—I was not going to get a new pair. These shoes were my only option.

I wore my stitched up, ugly shoes every day for at least six months, but I would hide my shoe's flaw. When sitting, I would cross my feet, so my right shoe covered my left. When I stood, I would position my left shoe in back of me to hide its flaw. I worked hard to conceal my shoe's flaw, but I was not as good as I thought. My friends would always see the flaw and ask me what happened to my shoe.

Eventually, I got tired of hiding the flaw on my shoe. Hiding our flaws requires a good amount of intentionality and is mentally exhausting. Hiding is not a viable and sustainable option for us to live out for the rest of our lives.

Surrendering My Pain

I needed to surrender the emotional pain I felt from the divorce to God because the pain was making me sick. I desperately wanted to get to the other side of my pain but didn't know how. What was I supposed to do with the grief, sadness, feelings of rejection, betrayal, and abandonment?

I decided to reach out for help but didn't know where to start. I felt too embarrassed to talk with anyone from my church. Going to counseling would probably help, but I didn't want the type of counseling I'd had before. I wanted to move beyond talking about the divorce and my emotional feelings of blame, shame, and grief. I desired to have a deep level of healing that would only come from a person trained in the ministry of healing emotional wounds based upon biblical principles.

That something different came in a way I would have never imagined. As I was walking through my season of grief, there was also a sprinkle of joy—my sister's wedding. Shortly after the wedding, she invited me to a women's conference at her new church. I decided to go. I wanted to support her because she didn't know any of the other women attending. I thought I was helping my sister by attending the conference, but it turned out God had a divine plan waiting for me.

During the second day of the conference, the speaker talked about Eve from the Bible. I'm not sure what specifics the speaker said about Eve because I became distracted by someone talking to me, not audibly but in a quiet, inner voice. That someone was the voice of God. Although I was not accustomed to him speaking to me, I knew it was him.

"You need to get to know her," God whispered in my ear.

I responded back in my head, "Get to know who?"

"The speaker. She has something for you."

I would never have thought the speaker and I had anything in common. We were of different ethnicities and walks of life. How could she help me?

Although I had my doubts about the speaker, I was still drawn to her. Also, because God had told me she had something for me, I was curious to find out what. During a break, I rushed over to the speaker and introduced myself. She told me her name was Lucy.

We exchanged a few pleasantries, and then I said, "God told me I needed to get to know you, but I don't know why. I'm dealing with some emotional pain right now and I'm wondering if you can help me. Are you a counselor?"

"Yes, I'm a biblical prayer counselor." She explained she counseled people through prayer and partnering with the Holy Spirit's leading. I didn't need to hear anything else. I was convinced God had sent her to help me. I knew I needed something different, and Lucy was going to help me discover that something.

The Power of Surrendering

When we surrender everything to God, including our emotions and pain, we open our hearts to a deeper level of intimacy and friendship with God. What does this deeper level of intimacy and friendship look like? The "going deeper" process for me involved deprogramming my thoughts on how I defined and encountered God's love. First John 4:18 (TPT) says, "Love never brings fear, for fear is always related to punishment. But love's perfection drives the fear of punishment far from our hearts. Whoever walks constantly afraid of punishment has not reached love's perfection."

I decided to do an exchange with God. I would give him my fear in exchange for his perfect love.

I practiced being intimate with God by sharing the issues of my heart and becoming authentic with him. I felt God wooing me to go deeper. Every evening, I would go into my secret place (my time of prayer and meditation) as Psalm 91 instructs us, and God and I would spend quality time together.

Initially, I felt uncomfortable talking to him like I would a friend. One evening when I was reading Psalms 91—our promise for God's help and protection when we're afraid—I heard the voice of God speak to me again, the same way he did at the women's conference. This time he asked me a question.

He asked, "Do you trust me?"

My immediate response was, "God, of course I trust you." Then truth and authenticity stepped in, and I changed my response. "No, God, I don't trust you completely. I trust you with the easy things in my life—the 80 percent—but when it comes to the hard things—the 20 percent—I don't trust you."

The truth of my inability to trust God was hard to admit, but I knew he desired truth from me. I would hold no more secrets from God. My goal was to become vulnerable, authentic, and truthful in every area of my life.

When I was in my secret place with God, I felt safe and at peace. The more intimate time I spent with God, the more I learned about his character and his love for me. As I started to fall in love with God, I experienced more of his unconditional love, and I began to trust him—really trust him with everything. I felt a new freedom to let it all go and to surrender everything I still held on to. This included my not-so-perfect life, my disappointments about the divorce, my past mistakes, my fear of the future, my control, my temper tantrums, my anger, and my pain.

Get Up, Girl, Let's Go Exercise:

Starting today, go on a no-negative-talking fast—only talk about any negative things with God and not with anyone else. When we stop talking negatively, our thinking will also line up. What negative talk about yourself can you throw into the trash can?

What are three positive things you know God loves about you?

Think about God saying this to you: "Daughter, today I want to shift your perspective and give you a fresh understanding of who I am. I want you to understand I love you, and I am here for you no matter how your circumstances change from day-to-day. I know things happened this week that set you off, and you are questioning why. You stood up for what was right, held your tongue, prayed, forgave, shared me with a coworker, and did not overspend. But things are still so wrong.

"Everything you did are great things, but I want you to understand the biblical model of love is based upon my covenant with you and not your performance. You do not have to express your love for me by what you do for me. I want you to love me and receive the unconditional love I have for you. Your mind has been set on things working out for your good based upon your performance, but that is not how I operate. Life is more than checking off all the boxes and feeling satisfied for tasks completed. Although you feel you are doing everything right, it is not going to provoke me to love you more, move quicker to rescue you, heal you, or give you a gold star for a job well done.

"Your life is in my hands. I am directing it because I see what is ahead of you. I want to position you for success. Your job is to get to know me and learn to trust me completely. I don't want to just be your God in general. Invite me into your day-to-day life—the triumphs and the drama. This is where you will find me and learn who I am to you. I can handle the truth. You do not have to suck it up for me. Your thoughts, fears, emotions, and struggles do not scare me.

"Think about how you can start aligning your perspective with mine and move in that direction. If I'm leading you away from something, don't try to hold on to it. Likewise, if I'm leading you toward something, don't try to run away. I want our relationship to be like a current is to water. I am the current, and you are the water. The water must submit to the current. Allow me to move you where I want to take you. Sometimes the movement will be gentle, and other times it will be forceful, leading you into stormy and rocky places crashing up against you. Relax because I am in control of the current. Do not go against the direction I am taking you. Doing so will cause waves in your life that will make you dizzy. Also, if you go against the direction I am taking you, you will not be able to receive the peace and rest I want to give you. I keep you moving for a reason. I do not want you to become like a stagnant and stale pond where mosquitoes fester, and algae grow. That is not a fruitful place, and I want your life to bear much fruit.

"As you surrender to the current, we can develop a good relationship, and you can learn more things about my character. I'm a loving and trusting God who is working everything out for your good."

God, today I am surrendering my negative thoughts at your feet. Would you please take them and replace them with positive thoughts about your love for me and who you have created me to be? I want to move forward, fulfilling my God-created purpose. I no longer give in to being stuck with distractions which keeps me focused on things not in my control and not important to you.

Reflection:

What distractions in your life are consuming your time and preventing you from developing a closer relationship with God?

Action:

Write and pray Matthew 6:33 over yourself, inserting your name:

"Seek the Kingdom of God above all else, and live righteously, and he will give you everything you need."

Example:

Seek the Kingdom of God above all else, Tracy, and live righteously, and he will give Tracy everything she needs.

CHAPTER 5

Negative Thoughts and Emotions

The average person processes 70,000 thoughts per day.[1] The Bible says in Proverbs 23:7 (NKJV), "For as he thinks in his heart, so is he." In other words, if the majority of our 70,000 thoughts are negative, we shouldn't be surprised if our lives are also negative. Likewise, if most of our thoughts are positive, we will have positive lives. Our thoughts are powerful.

Negative thoughts can stick with us for years. Those thoughts become our battles, issues, insecurities, and may be the reason we remain stuck. In the book, *Stand and Deliver*, Tim and Beth Scott define a mind stronghold as a demonic fortress of thoughts. They are:

1. Controlling, dictating, influencing our thoughts, attitudes, and behaviors.
2. Oppressing and discouraging us.
3. Filtering and coloring how we view and react to situations, circumstances, or people.[2]

Learning from the Scott's and other teachings, I understand mind strongholds are established through deliberate deception and plans devised by the devil to keep us stuck in negative cycles and thinking patterns.

The deceptive part is we believe these strongholds define us because they have been part of us for as long as we can remember. They may even be generational.

In the life map exercise in chapter two, you highlighted some events that have shaped you into the person you are today—events both challenging and beneficial. These events helped form your thinking, defined how you view life, and contributed to how you communicate and show up in relationships. In addition, your life map is your guide in showing some not-so-obvious negative cycles and patterns possibly hindering you from healing and walking into complete freedom in every area of your life.

Strongholds can keep us stuck in a cycle that prevents us from moving forward. The cycle starts with a negative thought, which partners with a negative emotion, which produces a negative action, and then the cycle repeats itself. Once we learn how to recognize and identify any mind strongholds and negative thought patterns, we can start to get unstuck. Let's explore how these negative thoughts, emotions, and actions can show up in us.

Negative Thoughts

Here are four categories listing sixteen common negative cycles and thinking patterns that might be keeping you stuck.

Category 1: Negative cycles/thinking in your relationship with yourself

- Overthinking—catastrophizing, expecting the worst.
- Deep insecurities—low self-esteem, concerned about how others perceive your words and actions. Fearing rejection.

- Being critical of yourself—I'm not good enough. I don't like my chin, nose, hair, etc.
- Procrastination—not able to finish what you start. I can't be perfect, so why try?

Category 2: Negative cycles/thinking in romantic relationships

- Experiencing hurt repeatedly.
- Volatile relationships with explosive anger, yelling, throwing things.
- Codependency—overly concerned with other's feelings and needs, patient with others but criticisms and doubts about yourself.
- Controlling/Manipulative Behavior—love is withdrawn if the other person does not meet expectations.

Category 3: Negative cycles/thinking with family and friends

- Seeking approval—need others to agree with you. You can't feel good about yourself without the support and affirmation of others.
- Lack of boundaries—unable to say no. I don't like this. This is a nonnegotiable for me.
- Enabling behavior—not allowing others to accept the consequences for their actions, offering a pillow each time they stumble or fall.
- Comparison/Jealousy—doesn't allow me to love myself.

Category 4: Negative cycles/thinking with God

- Manipulating God—he is a genie in a lamp. Only interact with him when you need something.
- Anger/Blame—God, why did you allow it?

- Conditional love—I am accepted and loved by God if I check all the boxes of how Christians should act.
- God doesn't care about my emotions—he sees them as weakness and sin.

Are there any negative cycles/thinking you notice in your relationship with yourself?

Are there any negative cycles/thinking you notice in your romantic relationships?

Are there any negative cycles/thinking you notice in your family and friend relationships?

Are there any negative cycles/thinking you notice in your relationship with God?

Negative Emotions

After my first session with Lucy, the good Christian girl view I had of myself came to a screeching halt. Lucy challenged my thinking and encouraged me to go deeper in my relationship with God.

One day during our session, Lucy told me, "We're going to have to deal with the fear in your life."

I'm sure the expression on my face revealed both surprise and disbelief. Although I didn't understand her statement completely, I could discern the implication wasn't good. I also felt offended because she saw something weak or insufficient about me. My natural response when I feel criticized is to defend my case.

"But I'm not afraid of anything," I told her. "My name means fighter, and I'm living my name! I won't pick a fight but I sure know how to defend myself if someone starts one with me."

Lucy politely responded to my rebuttal with a smile. I could not see how fear was operating in my life. I decided to put her comment in the parking lot in my head and maybe process it later. After several months of counseling with Lucy, the later moment came. I started to see the impact of what the many years of rejection had produced in me.

Negative Actions

Lucy encouraged me to view my life as a fruit tree. The soil in which my tree is planted represents the damaging events in my life. Suppose my soil includes damaging events like rejection, abandonment, divorce, violence, abuse, illness, disaster, or negative parenting. These events get into my tree's root system and can produce bitter roots in me—vows, negative feelings, judgments, unforgiveness, dishonesty, disrespect, and fear. As my tree grows, my bitter root responses form wrong beliefs and lies about myself, God, and life in general. Wrong beliefs produce bad fruit or unwanted behavior in my life which can also be sinful responses. Here is the tree and the types of fruit wrong beliefs and lies about us produce:[3]

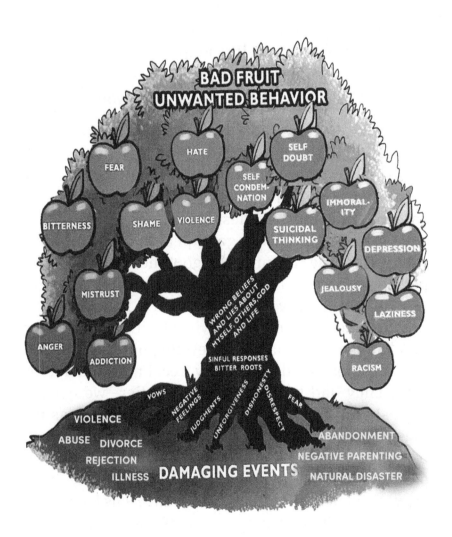

- Reflect on your life map you completed in chapter 2. Review the list of damaging events in the soil of the tree pictured above. Circle the ones you relate to (for example: rejection, abuse, divorce).
- Reflect on your life map and review the list of bitter root responses. Circle the ones you relate to.
- Reflect on your life map. What bad fruit or unwanted behavior have you seen in your life? Circle which ones might apply to you.

In Luke 6:43–45, Jesus teaches a parable about fruit in people's lives. The Scripture says, "A good tree can't produce bad fruit, and a bad tree can't produce good fruit. A tree is identified by its fruit. Figs are never gathered from thornbushes, and grapes are not picked from bramble bushes. A good person produces good things from the treasury of a good heart, and an evil person produces evil things from the treasury of an evil heart. What you say flows from what is in your heart."

After Lucy shared the tree visual with me, I realized I had a long list of damaging events, bitter responses/sins, and unwanted fruit on my tree. I now understood what Lucy had told me months earlier—we needed to deal with the fear in my life because fear was the biggest piece of fruit on my tree. The fear seeds had been planted when I was ten years old through cycles of rejection. They produced deep roots causing me to view my identity through a performance lens focused on what others thought and needed instead of through the lens of how God saw me and what he needed from me.

Fear Cycle

We can all agree about what fear looks like from the outside. We see the face of fear when we watch a scary movie, or when we see a spider (or a mouse, in my case), or when we must speak in public. The response to fear is typically a scream, a wince, widened eyes, or sweating profusely. However, the not-so-obvious fear we can't always see is the fear we carry inside of us.

I didn't realize my relationship with fear until Lucy started working with me on facing what I feared the most: breaking up with my fearful parts. For years, like Tar, Fear had become my friend. Fear had protected me for years, helped me hide my insecurities and broken parts, and never repeated any of our secrets. She would tell me which mask to wear when I needed to hide. She would also let me know the people I needed to avoid and with whom I should never share my heart. She taught me the issues of my heart were between me and her only. As time went on, Fear's voice became more prominent and controlling. She would tell me to shut up and demanded perfection from me. She taught me I should never raise my voice or show the emotions of anger or sadness. According to her, those emotions were terrible, and they would cause people to label me as not being "spiritual" enough.

Fear reminded me my thoughts, feelings, likes, and dislikes didn't matter. I learned to obey Fear. I became a woman who didn't express her emotions or feelings. I stuffed them instead.

When I did get the courage to speak about my pain, Fear judged me and told me I should be content and not complain because I had a good life. Fear didn't encourage me to establish healthy boundaries with others. Instead, I was encouraged to please people by taking responsibility for other people's lives and my own life. Fear's high expectations of me kept me on the tight wire of performance. If I slacked in any way, she would immediately let me know areas in my life that needed improvement and growth.

How has fear shown up in your life? How has fear protected you? What is your relationship with fear? What has she taught you?

I finally started to see the truth about Fear. I was not operating in honesty with myself, God, and others about the issues of my heart. I only knew myself by my roles: wife, mother, daughter, sister, and employee. I didn't know who I was outside of my titles.

Fear encouraged me to create and live a false identity and I fed the voice of Fear by avoiding, hiding, and trying to figure out my own issues. Finally, all my broken parts were staring me in my face, and I had no other option but to do what I feared most—I had to break up with Fear, let go of control, and fully surrender to God.

Review your life map. In what seasons have you experienced emotional pain? How long have you been carrying this pain?

Anger Cycle

We can carry emotional pain for years. It can slowly become an integral part of life, eventually impacting our personalities and decisions. Emotional pain can weigh us down and cause us to become victims of pain, causing us to avoid it or pretend it doesn't exist. Unaddressed or suppressed pain, however, will always show up later in our life with more intensity than before. This happened to a woman named Carol who came to me for mentoring and coaching.

When Carol filed a complaint about her boss's unprofessional conduct, she started experiencing unfair treatment. She had followed all the rules and done what she perceived to be right, yet her "right" was rewarded by rejection. The rejection came in the form of not receiving affirmation for the job she was doing well. Instead, she mostly heard what needed to be corrected in her job performance. Carol tried to bypass her feelings of not being valued or understood by working harder and trying not to be overly sensitive. Within months, Carol's fun-loving and confident personality became insecure, angry, and vindictive.

Carol wasn't a Christian, but one day I asked her if she would like to start praying together about her situation, and she immediately said yes. For months, we prayed together, asking God to help her let go of angry and vengeful thoughts. We asked God to provide strength, peace, and the wisdom for the right solution. Our prayer time led to us beginning a weekly Bible study. Carol found a great deal of peace as we prayed and studied the Bible together. Soon, Carol invited Jesus Christ into her heart to become her Lord and Savior.

After Carol accepted Jesus as her personal Savior, I noticed her anger and desire for revenge decreased as God began filling the empty spaces of her heart with joy and peace.

Carol grew in her relationship with Jesus as she studied the Bible and realized God had an answer for all her fears and concerns. Her transformation was a joy to watch.

One day, I asked Carol if she was interested in walking through the life map exercise. She agreed, and I asked her a few questions about her childhood. Her responses were open and honest, but suddenly, she grew quiet and then started to cry.

"My mother never gave me the approval I needed," she told me. "She always had very high and unrealistic expectations of me from very early childhood and all through my life."

Carol had never experienced the close mother/daughter bond because of the rejection she experienced when she was in her mother's presence. The lack of love and emotional support from her mother caused Carol to develop anger and resentment toward her mother which she still held onto even though her mother had died.

Carol immediately recognized the discord she was experiencing in her job was rooted in the unresolved pain she felt in her relationship with her mother. The feelings of not being appreciated, accepted, or valued on her job were the same feelings she'd experienced in her mother's presence.

Carol had been carrying this pain for over forty years.

She also realized this unhealthy rejection cycle was now showing up as a generational pattern—evident in the relationship she had with her son. To make sure he was a strong, confident decision-maker who would steer clear of the same mistakes she had made, she'd become a micro-manager, unknowingly perpetuating the cycle of rejection.

Shame and Guilt Cycle

Have you ever felt God would never forgive you for a mistake you've made? One of the heaviest burdens we can carry is the weight of feeling shame and guilt. Although the emotions of shame and guilt might seem similar, they look different in our lives.

Shame is an emotion focusing on what is wrong with me. We experience shame when we examine our faults, failures, and poor decisions and then judge ourselves as not good enough. We also shame ourselves when we don't live up to an expectation. Shame tells us we don't deserve love because we need to be a better person. Shame convinces us to hide our past and create a secret life.

On the other hand, guilt is an emotion which says I did something wrong. It focuses on how I have failed at something or how I did something wrong to someone else. Guilt focuses on our actions. Shame focuses on our personhood.

In John 8:1–11, we read about a woman caught in the act of adultery by the Pharisees. Jesus was nearby teaching in the temple courtyard, and people were gathered around him. The Pharisees brought the woman who had been caught in the act of adultery and made her stand in the middle of everyone. They wanted to shame her more. They said to Jesus, "The law of Moses says to stone her. What do you say?"

Jesus initially ignored them by bending down and writing something in the dust with his finger. The Pharisees insisted Jesus answer them. I love Jesus's response to these religious, law-following Pharisees. Jesus said to them, "All right, but let the one who has never sinned throw the first stone!" Jesus then bent over again and wrote more in the dust.

I wonder what Jesus wrote in the dust with his finger. Maybe, he noted each of their sins, because one by one, they walked away until all the woman's accusers had left. Jesus then does the most loving act—he stands and says to her, "'Where are your accusers? Didn't even one of them condemn you?'

'No, Lord,' she said.

And Jesus said, 'Neither do I. Go and sin no more.'"

In essence, Jesus told her she no longer had to be held hostage to her past.

Jesus is saying the same to us. He isn't shaming us like the Pharisees and desiring us to be guilty. If Jesus isn't shaming us or making us feel guilty, we shouldn't hold on to any shame or guilt either.

Get Up, Girl, Let's Go Exercise:

Look at your list of negative cycles/patterns as well as the unwanted behaviors and fruit you've circled on your tree. What would it mean for you to continue to hold on to all the cycles/patterns and the unwanted behaviors and bad fruit circled?

Can you identify with the woman caught in adultery in any way?

List five things you like about yourself.

How can you encourage yourself to silence your harsh inner critic thoughts?

How many times have we all said, "I don't care about what other people think"? The truth is we care deeply about what other people think about us. We adjust what we say and how we say it. We change our schedules and our behaviors to be perceived positively and to accommodate others. Sometimes our actions are not authentic and from the heart, but instead based upon expectations or duty. At times, we look for others to tell us we're okay. If others around us are okay, then we're okay.

There is nothing wrong with wanting others to be okay. The problem comes when we feel it's our responsibility to make them that way. If we're motivated by pleasing others and our actions and expectations of others become performance based, that is problematic.

A performance-based mindset never reaches the top of the performance criteria because the bar keeps getting placed higher and higher. Eventually, we become frustrated because we get tired of holding things together for others when we're not okay. How do we get out of the pit of performance?

Others might be pleased with our performance, but what about God? He doesn't want our relationship with him to be based upon a performance standard. He wants us to experience and encounter him by getting to know him on a deep, intimate level.

As we pursue a deep relationship with him, we discover our identity which is in him. God wants his love to penetrate us so profoundly we are set free from doing things out of duty or expectation. God wants our love for him and others to be based upon because-I-love-you unconditional love. We become good enough because of God's love for us. It is freeing to know our acceptance and lovability does not come from what we do or how well we do it. God's love covers all our fear, guilt, shame, and self-condemnation. When we feel loved, we can trust God over our fear, guilt, and shame. God's love meets us where we are. The love of God has transforming power to shift us into a new way of thinking.

Reflection:

Imagine you and God are having a conversation right now. What would you tell him about your negative cycles/patterns, fear, abuse, guilt, and shame? Close your eyes and listen to what he might say back to you. What would it mean for you to let them all go? In other words, release them and don't try to fix or hold on to them any longer. Write a prayer of release to God and specifically tell him what you want him to take control of in your life. Include all negative thinking, negative cycles, emotions, and actions you have identified as well as patterns and cycles in your life.

My Prayer of Release

PART TWO: LET'S GO

CHAPTER 6

Turning It All Over to God

Now that I've dug up all my issues, what do I do with all this stuff?

Our journey so far has been focused on challenging ourselves. The Get Up sections have helped us identify and recognize areas in our lives where healing is needed. These sections have also helped us consider new ways of thinking about our stuck areas. The Girl sections have inspired us to speak to ourselves in encouraging and loving voices that remind us to keep moving forward. In the Let's Go sections, we have engaged our spiritual self, reminding us God is with us always. He is intricately concerned about our success. He wants to help us get and remain unstuck and to become the God-created version he intended.

We have also explored where we might be stuck. We faced our past, processed surrendering control, and learned the impact of negative thoughts and negative emotions.

Take a deep breath. Hug yourself and pat yourself on the back because you have done some amazing work to discover some important treasures about your story.

I'm sure you've recognized there were events in your life where you didn't think you were going to make it. You were emotionally done, ready to move on, but didn't have the strength to do so. There were also some stuck places deeper than you thought, places where you needed some additional strength to overcome.

To this point, we've dug deep, explored, investigated, and opened wounds from our past. Now all this stuff is out in the open for us to see. What are we supposed to do with it all? There's only one totally effective solution—turn it all over to God. He is the only one who can completely heal and restore us.

"Well," you ask, "how do I do that?"

I'm so glad you asked.

How Do I Give It All to God?

In chapter three, we defined what it means to surrender to God—giving up on trying to figure out life's issues on our own. Instead, we've decided to concede to God's way of working things out, without trying to force our own solutions. Yielding means giving up control to any situation.

Oftentimes we are frustrated, disappointed, and overwhelmed by our circumstances. Have you said to yourself, "I can't do this anymore," or have you had thoughts of giving up on solving your issue? If so, don't feel guilty or ashamed. This is a sign that you've come to the end of yourself, which is a good thing. Now you're ready to release the control of managing and solving the issue to God.

Become Acquainted with God Personally

King David's life was filled with adventure—drama, trauma, bad mistakes, running for his life ... the list goes on and on. Through it all, he learned where his true help came from. In Psalm 46:1, David declares, "God is our refuge and strength, always ready to help in times of trouble." David also says in Psalm 121:1–2, "I look up to the mountains—does my help come from there? My help comes from the LORD, who made heaven and earth!" When he was in a tough spot, David realized the help he needed could only come from God.

Jesus Gives us Access to the Father

Romans 5:1–2 says, "Therefore, since we have been made right in God's sight by faith, we have peace with God because of what Jesus Christ our Lord has done for us. Because of our faith, Christ has brought us into this place of undeserved privilege where we now stand, and we confidently and joyfully look forward to sharing God's glory."

Jesus said in John 14:6, *"I am the way, the truth, and the life. No one can come to the Father except through me."*

It is only through faith in Jesus we have access to the God the Father in heaven.

Sin blocks our access to God. We owed for our sins, but Jesus paid the debt we never could have paid. He took on our liability for our sins when he died on the cross. Jesus became the complete and final sacrifice for our sins. It is through Jesus's death and resurrection our broken relationship with God is restored.

In chapter five, I shared Carol's story. Her life began to shift as she surrendered to Christ and allowed him to take 100 percent control. Carol told me she felt desperate to see some changes in her life. She needed help. Although she had no idea what her life would be like if she surrendered to Jesus, she rationalized the result had to be better than the pain she felt. Now, Carol's new life in Christ brings her a great amount of joy, peace, and hope. She has the help and strength to confront and heal from her past.

Possibly, you can relate to Carol's story. You may agree with her decision to not stay in a place of pain that spills over into other areas of your life. Maybe you've been searching for help and answers on how to move beyond your painful past but haven't found any sustainable solutions. I have a solution for you. The solution is to be restored to God through developing a relationship with Jesus Christ.

John 3:16 says, "For this is how God loved the world: He gave his one and only Son, so that everyone who believes in him will not perish but have eternal life."

Our relationship with Jesus starts when we believe and confess him as the Son of God, and we invite him to become the Savior and Lord of our lives.

Are you willing to open your heart to Jesus's love? If you have not yet asked Jesus to come into your heart, but you desire to be in a relationship with him because of what he has done for you, here is a simple prayer you can recite aloud to invite him into your life:

> Jesus, I believe you are the Son of God, that you died on the cross to rescue me from sin and death and to restore me to the Father. I choose now to turn from my sins, my self-centeredness, and every part of my life that does not please you. I choose you. I give myself to you. I receive your forgiveness and ask you to take your rightful place in my life as my Savior and Lord. Come reign in my heart, fill me with your love and your life, and help me to become a person who is truly loving—a person like

you. Restore me, Jesus. Live in me. Love through me. Thank you, God. In Jesus' name I pray. Amen.[1]

If you have given your life to Jesus, but you would like to have a deeper relationship with him, here is a simple prayer to ask for a deeper relationship:

Dear Lord, I humble myself before you and confess my sin. I want to thank you for hearing my prayer and helping me return to you. Lately, I've wanted things to go my own way. I pray for guidance as I listen for your voice. Let me return to what is most important—you. Help me turn to you and find the love, purpose, and direction I seek. Help me to seek you first. Let my relationship with you be the most important thing in my life.[2]

Congratulations! Jesus is now living in your heart. Your new life in Christ has begun. Welcome to the family of God.

Journal your reflections or what you might have heard in your heart after you prayed:

How Do We Access God's Strength?

God's strength is activated in us when we are weak, when we need help, and when we ask for it. God has the power to step into our circumstances and supernaturally do, finish, and shift what we can't accomplish in our natural strength. For example, the apostle Paul felt weak and needed God's help. God told him something surprising. Instead of zapping Paul with supernatural assistance, God's reply to Paul's plea was, "My grace is always more than enough for you, and my power finds its full expression through your weakness" (2 Corinthians 12:9 TPT). In essence, God encouraged Paul to keep coming to him with his weaknesses and his power would give Paul the strength for everything he would face.

The same will happen for us. It may seem counterintuitive but, God says our "weakness becomes a portal to God's power" (2 Corinthians 12:10 TPT).

Spend some time telling God about your weaknesses and how you need his help to take control and to activate more strength in you.

We Have Access to God's Promises

Below are two Scriptures containing promises from God about the good things he is working in us when we go through trials and tribulations. Read the following Scriptures. Speak them aloud. Circle the good things mentioned and underline the conditions which apply to receive the good things.

Scriptures:

James 1:12—"God blesses those who patiently endure testing and temptation. Afterward they will receive the crown of life that God has promised to those who love him."

James 1:2–5—"Dear brothers and sisters, when troubles of any kind come your way, consider it an opportunity for great joy. For you know that when your faith is tested, your endurance has a chance to grow. So let it grow, for when your endurance is fully developed, you will be perfect and complete, needing nothing. If you need wisdom, ask our generous God, and he will give it to you. He will not rebuke you for asking."

In James 1:12, we will be blessed if we remain patient while enduring testing and temptation. If we keep standing and keep trusting God regardless of our feelings or how bleak our circumstances look, we are promised a crown of life. This crown is a form of honor and recognition Jesus gives to those who faithfully serve and honor him. I don't know about you, but this queen wants her crown! This Scripture reassures us that everything we have gone through—the good, bad, and the ugly—is not in vain if we keep trusting God as we walk through it.

The story of Hagar in Genesis 16 is a beautiful example of how God kept his promises and helped a woman who was used, betrayed, rejected, and abandoned. Hagar, Sarai's Egyptian maidservant, was part of Abram and Sarai's desperate plan to have a child. God promised them a son, but ten years passed, and Sarai was still barren. Sarai grew tired of waiting for God to fulfill his promise so she decided she would help God by creating a substitute plan. Sarai's plan was to give Hagar to Abram as his concubine wife. He would sleep with her, and she would conceive a child for them. In biblical times, having your concubine bear your children was a common practice when the wife was not able to conceive. The children birthed by the concubine were considered the children of the wife.

Abram willingly slept with Hagar, and she did conceive a child. When Hagar's pregnancy was known, Hagar taunted her mistress, but Sarai was not having it. She began to treat Hagar harshly. Hagar fled into the wilderness to escape Sarai's abuse, becoming a pregnant single woman without a place to call home.

But at her lowest point, God was with her.

While in the wilderness, God sent an angel to encourage her and to tell her to go back to Abram and Sarai. He also promised Hagar the child she was carrying was a son, and his birth would have a spiritual purpose. The angel told her to call him Ishmael, which means "God hears."

Although the people closest to Hagar had turned on her, God hadn't. He came to rescue Hagar and to remind her he had heard and seen her pain. Hagar named the Lord who spoke to her, "You are the God who sees me [*El-roi*]." Then she remarked, "Have I truly seen the One who sees me?" Hagar was comforted to know God personally cared about her. She felt strengthened to go back to face the people who had caused her a great deal of heartbreak. Sounds crazy, but now she had a vision for her future. She wouldn't let anyone destroy the plans and purpose God had for her and her son. She had to return to fulfill God's plan for her life.

First Peter 5:10 says, "In his kindness God called you to share in his eternal glory by means of Christ

Jesus. So after you have suffered a little while, he will restore, support, and strengthen you, and he will place you on a firm foundation."

Hagar's suffering activated God's grace to come and rescue her. The same God who rescued Hagar in her heartbreak is the same God who sees you and is ready and willing to rescue you too.

Can you relate to anything in Hagar's story? If so, what part?

How have you experienced God's grace when you needed help?

Do you need God to give you the strength to go back and face something? If so, tell God about it.

Is there a promise or word of comfort you desire to hear from God? If so, tell him what it is.

God I need comfort and a promise about:

We Have Access to the Holy Spirit—Our Helper and Comforter

What is the Holy Spirit's role? The role of the Holy Spirit is to help, guide, teach, and speak to us. He reveals all things, encourages us, gives us boldness, helps us become like Jesus, and gives us inner strength. In Acts 1:8 Jesus says, "But you will receive power when the Holy Spirit comes upon you. And you will be my witnesses, telling people about me everywhere—in Jerusalem, throughout Judea, in Samaria, and to the ends of the earth."

Second Corinthians 3:17 says, "For the Lord is the Spirit, and wherever the Spirit of the Lord is, there is freedom." Because the Holy Spirit is living in us, we have the power to be free in every area of our lives.

We can ask the Holy Spirit to give us the power to forgive those who have wrongfully used us. We can also ask the Holy Spirt for the strength to leave our old way of thinking and to reveal the path God wants us to take for our future. If you desire the Holy Spirit to lead your life, you can make an intentional choice to walk by the Spirit, which means to walk in God's will instead of your own will. Invite the Holy Spirit to take control of your life each day.

Finding Your Special Place to Meet God Daily

In the book *Surrender to Love, Discovering the Heart of Christian Spirituality*, author David G. Benner makes this statement: "If our experience of God is limited to our thoughts about Him, we haven't encountered God yet."[3] This statement resonated with me because I wasn't sure if I had encountered God. I had beautiful thoughts about God. There were times when I was refreshed in God's presence. However, having an encounter like the one Paul had on his Damascus road journey (see Acts 9 and Acts 26) wasn't part of my testimony. Encountering God means we are meeting him in our emotions, and not only with our thoughts. We are giving him access to our heart, the place where God can heal, strengthen, and shift our thinking. Where does this meeting take place? What happens when we meet?

Psalms 91:1 refers to the place where we meet with God as the secret place. The secret place is not necessarily a physical location. Instead, it's where God invites us to meet with him emotionally. It's where we go to have alone time with God and create a personal connection with him.

How do you get to the secret place? It's simple, just desire to pursue a relationship with God and be intentional about turning your desire into actionable steps. The Bible encourages us to pursue this relationship by knocking, seeking, and drawing near to God.

> "Keep on knocking, and the door will be opened to you." (Matthew 7:7).

> "Seek me and find me" (Jeremiah 29:13).

> "Come close to God, and God will come close to you" (James 4:8).

The key is for us to initiate the process with God. We knock when we show up and say hello each day, we seek by reading what he has to say to us in the love letter he has written for us (the Bible), and we draw near to him by being intimate and vulnerable with him in our conversations.

What happens in the secret place? God has some special things for us in the secret place. Read the below Scriptures and circle the special things.

Those who come to him will be fed (See Psalm 22:26).

Those who thirst will be satisfied (See Matthew 5:6).

Those who listen for him will hear (See Matthew 11:15).

Those who come will be hidden in the secret place of his presence (See Psalm 31:20).

These Scriptures promise that we will be fed spiritually, satisfied emotionally, hear God's comforting voice, and be protected when we feel afraid, misused, abused, rejected, or abandoned. God's daughters are provided a special place where we can run in the middle of trouble or any time we choose.

Get Up, Girl, Let's Go Exercise:

God wants you to step into your new season as a seeker of his presence and a seeker of his will. Anything pulling you away from God is not coming from his heart. Is there anything or anyone hindering you from drawing near to God?

What can you do differently to step into your new season? Hebrews 12:2 (TPT) gives some suggestions. Read the Scripture aloud and underline what the Scripture says to do:

> "We look away from the natural realm and we focus our attention and expectation onto Jesus who birthed faith within us and who leads us forward into faith's perfection. His example is this: Because his heart was focused on the joy of knowing that you would be his, he endured the agony of the cross and conquered its humiliation, and now sits exalted at the right hand of the throne of God!"

Think about God saying this to you: "Daughter I see you! How I see you is different from how you see yourself. I see your strength, how you have had to fight, how you have cried yourself to sleep asking and pleading for me to show up! I see how situations have come into your life and tried to devour and demolish your inheritance, your identity, your peace, and more importantly make you doubt that I am your God, the God who steps in and strikes down anything that tries to touch you!

"I see you and now it's time for you to see me. Look up my daughter, come up higher so you can be seated with me in heavenly places. No more distractions to block your view of me. For I am the God who works the possible out of your impossible circumstances. Expand your vision because I want you to see more of me. More of my love for you, more of my grace being sufficient, for I am enough, I am all you need. In your next level and season, you will see me as your good Father. The Father who loves you. No more assuming how I will move in your life. Allow me to be God, allow me to refine your vision to see me in all my glory, full of grace and compassion for you. I am the Father who dries up all your tears and the God who positions you for success. You will win the battle for your families, you will win the battle over your circumstances, you will win the battle for your destiny because I have stepped in and everything, everything, everything swarming around you will stop because I have commanded it to."

Reflection:

God is extending an invitation to you to go into the secret place. Where can you designate as your secret place to meet with God? How can you make your secret place special?

CHAPTER 7

Discovering Your True Identity

When you look in the mirror what do you see? Do you like your reflection or are you your own worst critic? Research indicates 80 percent of women over the age of eighteen are unhappy with the image they see in the mirror.[1] Research also reveals American women between the ages of eighteen and seventy-eight will spend nearly a quarter of a million dollars on their appearance in their lifetime to try to change what they don't like about themselves.[2,3] We want to display a positive image and look our best so we appear to be the best. Social media pages are filled with people who appear to have perfect lives—perfect hair, perfect bodies, and perfect relationships.

Is our image the real reason we don't enjoy looking in the mirror?

I believe our image issues play a key role in why we do not understand our true identity.

If you researched the word identity, you would get many definitions, categories of the word, and unique perspectives about what it means for various people and groups. For example, a psychological perspective defines identity as one's self-image, one's self-esteem, and individuality. However, a sociological perspective defines identity as a person's role in society. One's past, present, and future might influence identity. To add to the complexity of the definition, the word is also used in terms which imply one's identity can be lost, fraudulent, and cause a crisis. For example, identity theft means someone steals your identity. False identity means you are pretending to be something or someone you are not. And an identity crisis happens when there is confusion about one's sense of self.

One of *Merriam-Webster*'s definitions of identity is "the distinguishing character or personality of an individual."[4] *Yourdictionary.com*'s most popular definition of identity is "who you are, the way you think about yourself, the way you are viewed by the world, and the characteristics that define you." Another definition there is "the mask or appearance one presents to the world—by which one is known."[5]

I've heard people say, "I need to find myself." If I'm trying to find myself, does this mean somewhere along the way I've lost myself? If so, what have I lost? Has there been some major event or trauma that has stolen who I knew myself to be? Typically, if we lose something, our first response is to go back to the place where we think we've lost it and begin a wild search. In the same way, we often go back to the stuck places in our lives to find out why we lost our identity at the place.

Consider this: what if God didn't want you to go back to the place where you thought you lost your identity? What if he wanted you to shed the lost parts of your story because they have contributed to you being and staying stuck? Maybe God wants what you lost to stay lost because it won't serve you well in your future. Some of the things God wants us to lose are feelings of emptiness, discontentment, low self-esteem, loss of self-confidence, loneliness, anxiety, and depression. All these things can falsely attach to our identity and try to define us.

A strong sense of identity is essential for our health and well-being; it also helps us make decisions and know how to act and react in life. It helps guide where we should go for our future and gives us comfort, security, and belonging. A strong identity can help us get unstuck from our past, positively change our negative thinking, and end other cycles that have inhibited us from moving forward in our lives.

Our Two Identities

As Christians, we have had two births resulting in two identities. We had a natural birth as well as a spiritual birth. At our natural birth, we received earthly DNA and were given an earthly identity and genealogy. Likewise, through a spiritual birth—when we invite Jesus into our heart—we are given a heavenly identity, a heavenly genealogy, and heavenly DNA. Jesus explains the natural and spiritual birth processes in John 3:3–7. While having a conversation with Nicodemus, see what Jesus told him.

> "I tell you the truth, unless you are born again, you cannot see the Kingdom of God."

> "What do you mean?" exclaimed Nicodemus. "How can an old man go back into his mother's womb and be born again?"

Jesus replied, "I assure you, no one can enter the Kingdom of God without being born of water and the Spirit. Humans can reproduce only human life, but the Holy Spirit gives birth to spiritual life. So, don't be surprised when I say, 'You must be born again.'"

Also, John 1:12–13 says this about our spiritual birth: "But to all who believed him and accepted him, he gave the right to become children of God. They are reborn—not with a physical birth resulting from human passion or plan, but a birth that comes from God."

Although we have these two identities, we must decide which one is going to be our primary or true identity and which one will be our secondary identity. Which one is unstable? Which one is steadier? Which one brings us turmoil? Which one brings us peace? Which one is keeping us stuck? Which one can help get us unstuck?

Is Our Earthly Identity Our True Identity?

Our earthly identity is our natural or outward identity. It is how we might be described as a person. We use identifiers such as age, gender, nationality, and ethnicity to describe people. We can also be identified by our family background, relationship status, education, occupation, natural skills, giftings, and talents. It is interesting that our material possessions, such as our houses, clothes, and cars, as well as our difficulties, can often be used to paint a picture of our identity.

These earthly identifiers describe us and play a part in our role in society. Our earthly identity can change if our age, occupation, skills, or material possessions change. However, there are other aspects of our identity such as our ethnicity and family background we can never change. A strong earthly identity is important because it's connected to our self-esteem.

Because of our caretaker role as women, oftentimes our identities can be tied to how we care for our families, relationships, and our homes. There is nothing wrong with being caretakers. Our life has purpose and meaning when we are supporting others. The problems exists if our caretaker roles define our identity. What happens if the relationship ends? We do not quite know who we are without that person in our lives anymore. What happens when the children grow up? Mommy can suffer an identity crisis when she must identify with something else to make her feel useful and valuable again.

We must be careful to not allow our earthly identity to define us. The depth of who we are as women transcends our earthly identity. Our earthly identity can only describe us and never truly define us because it doesn't provide a complete picture of our inner value as women. If the criteria for us to discover our identity is solely based upon the earthly identifiers previously mentioned, our identity can constantly change.

The question arises, "Can I discover my identity if the foundation for my identity is constantly changing?" In my opinion, the answer to this question is no. If my identity is often changing, I would constantly be in an identity crisis mode. If someone asked me, "Who are you?" I would have to respond, "Do you mean who am I today?" A changing identity can cause us to have low self-esteem and feel unstable and insecure. We would also become self-absorbed and lack confidence.

Why? Because when things are constantly shifting and changing, it's difficult to be focused. We thrive and grow better when our lives are stable.

How have others described you based upon your earthly identity? Have these descriptions impacted your life? If so, explain.

Think of a comment someone once made over you (positive or negative) that ended up defining who you think you are today. Why do you suppose that comment had such an impact on you?

Is Our Heavenly Identity Our True Identity?

Our heavenly identity is our value as God sees us and what he says about us. It's what lies inside of us— the deeper side of us. This identity reflects our heart and our character. Our heavenly identity comes from God. It's our original identity, the God-created version of us. Jeremiah 1:5 mentions God knew us before he formed us in our mother's womb. God is the one who has given us our heavenly identity. God wants us to see our identity and our value as women based upon his perspective.

Differences Between Our Earthly and Heavenly Identities

Below are common questions about identity. Each question is answered based upon an earthly identity perspective and a heavenly identity perspective. Read each question and circle the response you can more closely identify with.

Common Identity Questions	Earthly Identity Response	Heavenly Identity Response
Am I responsible for creating my own identity?	Yes. Identity is based on my achievements, my education, and what I do for others—my role.	No. Identity is formed because of who I am in Christ—my position has already been defined. I don't have to do anything to earn it. It's founded in grace, not in my works, not determined by my performance.
How do others describe me?	How I look, my personality, my age, nationality, and sex.	I am a child of God, adopted, fearfully and wonderfully made.

Do my relationships give me my identity?	Yes. I'm at my best when I'm in a relationship.	Yes, my relationship with Christ is my first relationship, and from that relationship, I can have a deep and satisfying relationship with others.
How do you measure your value?	Approval from others, the amount of money I make, successful career, and relational status.	It's based on God's love. He loves me no matter what happens. His love will never change.
How is my identity formed?	Through discovering me, what I like, dislike, and following my heart. Influenced by life's experiences, what others have said about me, how I view myself, my interests. It's an ongoing process.	I received a new identity when I came to Christ. 2 Corinthians 5:17 says, "This means that anyone who belongs to Christ has become a new person. The old life is gone; a new life has begun."
Does my identity change?	Yes. It can change based upon my circumstances, how I might feel, or if I have a major life crisis.	No. It's rooted in God's love which never changes. It doesn't change when my circumstances change.

The Strategy to Steal Our Heavenly Identity

The topic of identity is important to God, so Satan wants us not to completely embrace our heavenly identity. His plot to confuse us about our identity began with Adam and Eve. They were in the garden enjoying God's fellowship, freely walking around naked and unashamed. Suddenly, guess who shows up? Satan disguised as a cunning serpent. He came to tempt Eve. Why? He wanted Eve to question her heavenly identity. The serpent tried to make her feel discontented and convince her she was missing out on something good in her life. Satan tried to convince her God was holding her back from tapping into her true identity.

Eve fell for the serpent's manipulative setup and began to question her heavenly identity. Her disobedience—and Adam's involvement in the same disobedience—resulted in breaking the intimate fellowship they had with God. Satan's deception started with Adam and Eve, and it continues with us today. His objective is to confuse us about our heavenly identity through our challenges.

As previously mentioned, when we come to Christ, we are new people and new creations in Christ Jesus. When we come to Christ, we have the right to shift from our old earthly identity to our new heavenly one.

Jesus Knew His Identity

For the three and half years Jesus ministered on earth, people tried to define his identity. Matthew 16:13–20 highlights a conversation Jesus had with his disciples about his true identity. He affirmed their answer—he is the Messiah. Jesus didn't allow what others assumed he was or what others said about him to change his mind about his heavenly identity.

Our heavenly identity is our true identity. What makes our heavenly identity our true identity? It's how God sees and defines us.

Heavenly Identity	Why Our True Identity?	Scripture
We belong to God.	God created us, and he knows us best.	Ephesians 1:13.
We are sealed with the Holy Spirit.	The Holy Spirit brands us as God's property.	Ephesians 1:13.
Our citizenship is in heaven.	We have eternal life. When Jesus returns, our earthly identity ends, our heavenly identity continues forever.	Philippians 3:20.
God's masterpiece.	God is creating our life into a piece of beautiful art. He is working on us and doing something special and good in us.	Ephesians 2:10.

Our heavenly identity is the most accurate and real of our two identities. It's not based upon *who* we are, it's centered around *whose* we are. It's our true and authentic identity because it's grounded in our relationship in Christ.

Adverse circumstances such as divorce, health challenges, or working through relational difficulties can be catalysts that cause us to question our heavenly identity and search for earthly solutions outside of God. God wants us to shift entirely into our heavenly identity and not teeter between our earthly and heavenly identities when we deal with difficult circumstances. When difficulties happen, invite God to come into the circumstance and get his perspective on the matter.

God is using everything we have been through to shape and grow our heavenly identity. The situations we go through might make us feel like we're having an identity crisis. However, God is working behind the scenes on our behalf, creating a come-back strategy to stabilize us beyond what we could never imagine.

I'll never forget when I was trying to find my identity after my divorce. One day, I told my counselor Lucy, "I can't wait to get to the other side of this mess."

Lucy said, "What if God is using this mess to shape you into the woman he wants you to be in the next chapter of your life?"

I had never considered how God might be using the divorce to mold me into my heavenly identity and create a new storyline for my life. He was shaping my heavenly identity to give me a new and powerful testimony to share with other women who have walked through a similar journey to mine.

Years ago, God told me that he wanted me to start a Bible study for women. I immediately said, "No. Not going to do that." I thought there was no way God was calling me to start a Bible study. That was my mother's calling and gifting, not mine.

My excuses seemed valid. I didn't know the Bible well enough to teach it, my personal life was in chaos, and truth being told, I didn't really get along with other women. I had a few good friends, but I wasn't sure if I wanted to let anyone else into my world.

After months of stalling, being afraid, and trying to figure out all the logistics, I finally gave in and started the "Women of Purpose" Bible study group on faith. I felt totally out of my comfort zone, but afraid to disobey a direct request from God.

For two years, a group of ten women committed to discovering the truth about our identity. We are all Christians, but each of us struggled with brokenness from our past. Our brokenness kept us stuck from moving forward in God's will to the next chapter he had for us. We were fearful, insecure, holding on to shame and guilt from our past, and just not clear on our true heavenly identity as Christian women. Together we took some bold steps to start a journey of discovering our true identity.

As we submitted to the process to allow God to redefine us, the layers of our earthly identity started to fall off, and we shifted into our heavenly identity. Here are some things we discovered as we walked through the process:

- The journey to true identity is a process. It took years to start seeing the fruit of our commitment.

- Shifting identities is necessary to pursue a deeper relationship with God. No more lukewarm Christianity, idol worship, being double-minded, or trying to walk in our understanding to stay in control would be tolerated.

- Obedience is essential. We didn't want to get ahead of God. We stopped driving and directing traffic. Instead, we allowed God to position us where he wanted to take us. We would no longer open our own doors or step in and try to make things happen.

- Our love for God and his love for us is based on a true, intimate relationship and not on performance. God invited each of us to allow him to heal us by his perfect love—his unconditional love. God's unconditional love is the foundation for our identity.

- Accountability and community made the process easy and fun. We would not have been able to take this journey to discover our true identity by ourselves. Smaller life teams within the larger group drilled down to more intimate levels of accountability. Life teams hold you accountable in how you want to grow and help you get there. We were surprised to discover the ways God used three of us to encourage, strengthen, and build each other's confidence to take some risks. Without each other's encouragement, the process would have been more challenging.

It's amazing to see what God has done in the lives of the women who attended that Bible study. We are now walking in our heavenly identities of applying our desires and giftings to advance God's kingdom in government, leading praise and worship in churches, publishing books, hosting talk shows, and more importantly being free from all self-imposed limitations that kept us emotionally stuck.

The Bible study ladies often laugh and reflect on the fact we had no idea what God was up to. We understood we were in a season of reconstruction. God was rebuilding us into a new and improved version of ourselves, the 2.0-God-created version.

The God-created version of you is the version that operates according to God's will and purpose for your life. Maybe you have discovered you have allowed your earthly identity and many outside influences to shape and create the woman you are today. Those influences were based upon your upbringing and the other roles you've learned to play in your personal experiences. Consider asking God how he sees you and what his meaning is for your life. Ask him for what purpose you were created.

Hopefully, you have decided you want your heavenly identity to be your primary identity. If so, now it's time to confirm and declare your heavenly identity by giving God your yes. Recite out loud the below yes statements:

- Yes, God, I want to see myself as you see me.

- Yes, God, I desire to understand and embrace my heavenly identity fully.

- Yes, God, I commit to being intentional about moving away from incorrect ways of thinking by not resurrecting old memories. I will let the dead things of my life stay buried.

- Yes, God, I will shift my thinking to only speak about myself according to how I'm defined in Scripture.

- Yes, God, I will take a risk and obey and trust you completely and allow you to transform me into someone new.

Do you believe God can shift your life into something good and meaningful? Romans 8:28 reminds us: "And we know that God causes everything to work together for the good of those who love God and are called according to his purpose for them." The good news is our heavenly identity doesn't require us to perform or to look for our life's solutions externally. The solution, peace, and rest we need is in our relationship with God.

Get Up, Girl, Let's Go Exercise:

Are there things you want to let go of regarding your earthly identity? Is there anything about your perceived self-worth keeping you stuck in fear and being unproductive? Based upon what you've learned about your heavenly identity, what are some specific ways you can adjust your thinking to align with how God sees you?

Say to yourself, "I am the complete package." I have everything I need in my relationship with God. I can now move forward knowing my value and my worth in the eyes of God. I am loved, favored, chosen, and I am more than enough. I am an adopted daughter accepted and not rejected.

Prayerfully read and reflect on the following devotion. Allow what God says about your heavenly identity to transform your thinking. Consider the power of God's unconditional love for you and how it alone can help shift your thinking about your heavenly identity. Allow his love to become the foundation for your identity.

What Do You Think About Me, God?

"Thank you for making me so wonderfully complex! Your workmanship is marvelous—how well I know it" (Psalm 139:14).

"Daddy, who am I, and what have you created me to be?"

God says, "Daughter, before I formed you in your mother's womb, I knew you. Before you were born, I set you apart for my glory and purpose to be a voice for me. The day you came into this world I looked at your face, and I fell in love. Here are my thoughts about you.

"You are a success. You are brave and gifted with purpose. Like a pure diamond, you are beautiful, radiant, and multifaceted. I marvel at the unique characteristics I gave you. I smile when you use your gifts for my glory. There are no limits to what you can achieve through me. I give you the strength to overcome every obstacle that comes your way. You are my workmanship—my handiwork, born anew in me to do my works.

"I delight in you. You should hear me talk about you. I am happy we have an intimate relationship in which we can share with each other. I know what you think, and I can finish your sentences. I have counted every hair on your head, and I keep a running tally. You want to know how many you've lost today? I care about what you care about—the things that make you frown and cause pain in your heart. I've bottled up every one of your tears. When we see each other, I'll show you all your bottles. All those ashy things that happened to you, I'm turning into something beautiful.

"You are my princess. You come from royalty. Don't forget—your daddy is the King. You have been granted certain privileges, and you have an inheritance—favor and eternal life, just to name two. My thoughts of you are for good and not for evil. Anything that comes your way must get my approval first. I am also your protector. When arrows are thrown at you, I step in front of them, so none touch you.

"You are my beautiful butterfly. Like the butterfly, I created you to transform. Your purpose is not to stay in a cocoon, be collected, or be stuck and stapled to a cardboard and put on display. You are free! I didn't create you to carry the burden of your sin or the sins of others. I paid the price. You don't need to hold on to any more grief. I created you to tell others how they can also be set free. If you don't fly with freedom, how will you encourage others to see the beautiful colors and grace my freedom gives? When others see the beauty of your freedom, they will be inspired to be free also.

"You are loved with an everlasting love. My love for you surpasses all other types of love you have experienced before. There is no human love comparable to my divine love for you. I will never leave you or forsake you because you are my Baby Girl. Nothing you could ever do would cause me to reject you. You can run far away from me, but I'll come after you. I've made plans to take care of you forever. I sent my son Jesus to die for you so we could spend eternity together. This is my unconditional love for you.

"My daughter of purpose, through me you have hope and a bright future. You can't see all the amazing things I have planned for you because of your current circumstances, but put your confidence in me, and I will complete the work I've started to do in you."

Reflection:

How can what God says and thinks about you shift your thinking about your identity?

CHAPTER 8

Trusting God and Others

Trust means believing in and relying on someone or something. In my opinion, the word *trust* is one of the most powerful words in the English language. This emotional word is powerful because it evokes a positive or negative response based upon one's relationship with the word. Just thinking about or saying the word trust can bring feelings of joy, peace, fear, anger, or sadness.

Trust plays a role in all kinds of things we do every day. We must have a level of trust when we walk outside our door. We trust others will be responsible to abide by the law. Without trust, we would stay isolated in our homes.

Trust is also the glue that holds a relationship together. Without trust, a relationship is doomed to fail. An unknown author said this about trust: "Trust takes years to build, seconds to break, and forever to repair."

Trust and the Issues of the Heart

We all have probably experienced a trust issue—a lack of trust with someone or something. Our negative or positive experiences have helped us decide if someone or something is trustworthy or not. Everyone is different in how and when they feel comfortable in trusting another person. For some, trusting another person comes easy, but for others trusting can be something developed over time or never obtained.

From the four choices below, write down what your experiences with God, family members, and romantic or friend relationships have taught you about trust. In row 5 feel free to add a specific person's name and what that relationship taught you.

Relationship	Lesson learned: To trust more, To trust less, To be suspicious, To be afraid
God	
Family Members	
Romantic Relationships	
Friendships	

When I travel, I don't eat salads with seafood. Twenty years ago, I traveled alone and I got a horrible case of food poisoning. I had to be admitted to the hospital. I still don't trust salads with seafood. The guiding principle of my life when it comes to seafood salad was cemented when I lost trust over a Shrimp and Crab Louis salad. Have you established any guiding principles for your life based upon lessons learned from any of your relationships?

Would you say trust has been your good friend or your worst enemy?

Developing a healthy relationship with trust is vital as it is foundational for our relationship with God and others. Not being able to trust can interfere with our ability to connect. Trust issues can also keep us stuck in hiding, where feelings of loneliness and isolation can develop. God did not create us to be alone—he created us to be in fellowship with others. To be in fellowship with others, we must be able to trust them.

How does one develop a healthy relationship with trust after being disappointed repeatedly? One way to develop a healthy relationship with trust is by becoming aware of and caring for the issues of our heart. They are the experiences that have hurt our heart, and issues that we have carried for years and just want to forget about.

What are the hurtful issues of your heart?

How long have you carried this issue?

What have you done with the hurtful things that have impacted your heart? Check any that apply.

- ☐ I don't think about them.
- ☐ I've done the work to address and deal with them.
- ☐ I'm working on them.
- ☐ I don't know what to do with them.

Some Christians believe they need to suck up the issues of their heart and pretend they don't exist. If we mask our heart issues and say God is going to deal with them, this can present a problem. Unprocessed issues of the heart can produce the fruit of mistrust, anger, depression, anxiety, nightmares, sleep issues, eating disorders, and the inability to have a confident sense of self-worth. Although we are new creations in Christ and we have a new heavenly identity, that doesn't mean we have to pretend and hide the things that have hurt us and still hurt us deeply. God wants us to be able to safely trust him and others with the things that have hurt our heart. God wants us to be free in expressing our heart issues. He doesn't want us to feel like we can't show the true condition of our heart or that we must maintain a strong and controlled image.

Our heart issues are not a sign of weakness but are actually a sign of strength. They indicate we are human, in touch with our emotions, and we care. Our heart issues are reminders from God about the things we need to address and possibly heal from. We can properly address our heart issues when we become aware of them.

I often ask the women I coach and mentor, "What are the issues of your heart?" The typical response I get is, "I'm not sure," or "I've never thought about it." God wants us to be mindful of our heart issues and trust him by discussing them with him. He can help us overcome the experiences and events that have caused our hearts to hurt the most.

If your heart could speak, what would it say about its issues?

A Trust Walk

A trust walk is a team building exercise to increase trust between two people. One participant is blindfolded and led by the other participant. The goal is to create a physically and emotionally safe experience for the partner who is walking without sight. The person being led must trust the person leading to be taken safely to a designated location. The person leading cannot touch the other person—the leader can only guide with their voice. Along the way, the two must maneuver around obstacles and ignore the loud noise, all designed to distract the blindfolded person and divert trust from the person leading. The winning team—the first to arrive at the designated location—is the team in which the follower most trusted the leader.

An Invitation to Go On a Trust Walk with God

I'll never forget one evening I was praying and asking God to show me the issues of my heart. I knew I had some issues because I could feel a heavy cloud over me—a cloud of disappointment and resentment that wouldn't go away. Also, my thinking wasn't right. My mind was filled with more negative thoughts than positive ones. I tried to figure out why I felt this way. I considered maybe I had these feelings because there was another level of trust God wanted to achieve in me, but I felt stuck. I knew God had a beautiful plan for my life, but something blocked me from seeing and trusting that plan.

After praying about my feelings, I fell asleep and had a dream. In the dream, Jesus and I stood on top of a mountain. The terrain was rocky, and I felt afraid. I asked Jesus, "Am I about to go through a wilderness experience again?"

Jesus grabbed my hand and said, "No. Actually, I'm going to guide you to the other side of this mountain where you will experience complete rest and joy. I'm taking you away from the rocky places." Jesus also explained he would be a few steps ahead of me, but to hold his hand tightly because we were going to leap across the mountain like gazelles. As we leaped across the mountain, I had the biggest smile on my face.

In this dream, God invited me to go on a trust walk with him. I mentioned in an earlier chapter when God asked, "Do you trust me?" My initial response was, "Yes, of course I do." But then I changed my response to, "No, I don't, I trust you 80 percent of the time." In the dream God highlighted the fact that I could trust him with the remaining 20 percent—where my trust issues lay. The stuck areas were places in my heart that I guarded to minimize any risks in my life. I controlled these areas to prevent myself from ever getting hurt again.

After the dream, I decided to do an exchange with God. I would give him my trust issues. Doubts, fears, disappointments, and resentments all went to him in exchange for trusting his plan for my life—a plan I could not see. I was willing to take the risk and trust him completely because I wanted to be completely set free and healed. Also, I couldn't stay in the place of pretending everything was fine anymore. I took the walk—my trust walk—with God, and that has made a tremendous difference in my life. Let me tell you about some other women who faced their heart issues by taking trust walks with God.

Trusting God after Infidelity

Sheila was married to the love of her life at the age of twenty-five. After five years of marriage, Shelia discovered her husband had been unfaithful. In addition to dealing with her husband's infidelity, Sheila, who had been trying to get pregnant, had experienced two miscarriages. Her life became frustrating and overwhelming. She developed trust issues with her husband as well as with God. She couldn't comprehend how her husband could betray her, and why God wouldn't allow her to conceive a child. She was stuck.

After Sheila and her husband separated, she asked God, "I assume you're releasing me from the marriage." She felt God's response to her was "No." He reassured her he would deal with her husband. He explained he had a bigger plan, a plan to restore her marriage. Shelia had to decide to either trust her plan, which was filing for divorce, or to trust God's bigger plan.

Sheila's Trust Walk

Shelia made the decision to take a gradual trust walk with God. She told God, "I'll know if I'm supposed to forgive my husband if he calls me and asks to come back by a certain date." Only she and God would know this date. And guess what happened? Shelia's husband did call her by that date. This was the confirmation she needed to take the complete step of trusting God, which meant working slowly toward forgiving her husband and allowing him to come back home.

But Sheila's trust and faith in her husband did not automatically strengthen with just that confirmation.

However, God promised Sheila he would mend her broken heart and help her move past the memories of rejection and betrayal. He instructed Shelia to "Forgive like I forgive." Sheila's response back to God was "I don't know if I can do that, and what does forgiving like you really mean?" He showed her that to forgive like God meant to let go of the grudges and anger she felt toward her husband and learn how to love him beyond his mistake. As she worked on forgiving her husband like God forgives, her life became a testimony for her husband's salvation. Soon, her husband invited Jesus to become his Lord and Savior. Sheila's trust walk involved learning how to forgive, but she also learned that forgiveness is a perpetual journey.

Trusting God When Others Hurt You

After five years of marriage to her best friend, Marie noticed her husband's patience getting shorter. When they argued, he became accusatory and jealous. One evening, they were having an argument. The next thing Marie knew, she could not see out of one eye. Her husband had hit her with so much force she lost partial vision in her left eye permanently.

Although she was a victim of domestic violence, Marie still loved her husband and prayed God would restore him and their marriage. Marie and her husband did not reconcile, however, and they eventually divorced. The most painful part of Marie's story was the subsequent work to reconcile the reasons why her best friend had hurt her.

Marie's Trust Walk

One of Marie's deepest trust issues was rooted in how she viewed her relationship with God. She viewed

God as a punisher—always waiting for her to make a mistake. This view came from how she experienced her earthly father.

Marie did not perceive God as someone who would be concerned about the everyday details of her life. Why would he care? After all, her choices disappointed her, so she perceived that God viewed her as a disappointment too.

Marie desired to have a deeper intimate relationship with God, but she wasn't convinced she could trust God or anyone else with all the issues of her heart. When her marriage fell apart, she felt she'd hit rock bottom. She decided to surrender herself to God and his trust walk instead of staying stuck in the negative space of betrayal and disappointment.

Instead of believing lies that blinded her from seeing and receiving God's character and good thoughts about her, she wanted to see the truth about his plans for her life. During her trust walk with God, through prayer and fasting, the Holy Spirit revealed to Marie she had been walking in her own understanding versus God's understanding for years. As Marie submitted to the process of going deeper in her relationship with God by giving up some incorrect thinking patterns, God began to deal with some of the deeper issues of her heart including:

- Mourning the loss of her best friend (her husband)
- Recovering from the physical and emotional hurt of the domestic violence incident
- Letting go of control and letting God lead
- Admitting she may never understand why the abuse happened
- Forgiving her ex-husband

- Letting go of the blame and guilt she piled on herself
- The need to change her perspective from a wounded one to a healed one

Marie's lack of trust toward God stemmed from not understanding her heavenly identity. Understanding who she was based upon God's perspective gave her the freedom to accept and forgive her past mistakes and believe they had nothing to do with how much God loves her now. She didn't need to keep him at a distance or hide her mistakes any longer. God was ready and willing to meet her where she was, brokenness and all. He extended his hand and invited her to receive his love.

Marie now enjoys being her authentic self with God. She trusts her secrets are safe with him. She has also learned the more she trusts God, the more she can trust others.

Trusting God When You Have Lost Hope for Your Future

Ann, a forty-two-year-old single woman, waited for God to send her a husband. Ann had two prior marriage proposals, each ending in a breakup. Both men had presented themselves as being committed, but each had betrayed Ann. She wanted to give up on the desire to be married, but deep down in her heart she didn't want to live her life alone. She prayed and asked God if it was his will for her to remain single, to give her peace and contentment about it, but peace never came.

Ann's Trust Walk

After the experiences with the two unfaithful people, Ann realized she had to be careful not to compromise or settle for less regarding the mate God had for her. However, she felt stuck. She didn't understand how to patiently wait on God's timing for her mate. Her feelings of being alone grew stronger. She could identify with Proverbs 13:12 which says, "Hope deferred makes the heart sick, but a dream fulfilled is a tree of life." Her heart felt sick, yet she continued to believe her dream of a mate would be fulfilled.

Ann didn't know how to trust God for her future spouse. She doubted God's word when he promised her good plans and a bright future for her life (Jeremiah 29:11). How would God find her husband, and did God need her help in doing so?

Ann read dating books encouraging single women to date many men to discover what they really wanted in a future husband. This pressure overwhelmed her because she was not accustomed to the dating game. Ann decided to try online dating. She met a man who she dated for a year, but then discovered he wasn't the right man for her. After that breakup, Ann felt done with the process of trying to help God find her husband.

One day, she drove behind a truck with a big sign that said, "Trust the struggle." In that moment Ann knew God was sending her a message. She heard him say, "Trust *me* in this struggle." She now felt convinced God was working something out although she couldn't see what it was. Ann's heart shifted and God gave her a new rest. Her anxious thoughts of finding a husband became serene thoughts as she waited on God.

While she was waiting on God for her husband, Ann discovered she needed to get busy living her life to the fullest. During this season, she wrote and published a poetry book and tapped into her creative side of painting and making crafts. She also got a new best friend—her dog baby Kole River. Ann fell in love with Kole, and he brought her companionship and love. Caring for Kole was just what Ann needed to heal her heart. Years later, Ann did meet the man of her dreams to whom she is married to today. God sent Ann his best designed just for her, but in his time and in his way.

Trusting God When Life Gets Hard and Challenging

It's easy to trust God when life is going great—the job is satisfying, relationships are healthy, and the future seems bright and promising. However, it's challenging to trust God completely when life throws us a curveball. The loss of a job, a health challenge, or betrayal by a friend or family member can open the door for doubt. We question if God can be trusted. We know God is good but is he reliable to support us in our personal challenges?

Trusting God extends beyond our beliefs and feelings. Trusting God means we choose to have faith in what God says although our circumstances and feelings try to convince us to believe something different. Trusting God means we can put all our weight and confidence in trusting him in every situation because he knows us best. He is concerned about our situation, our feelings, and the outcome.

It is within our difficult circumstances we can demonstrate if we really trust God. One way we can trust God is to invite him into every area of our lives, especially the challenging ones.

Your healing journey cannot progress until you are able to trust God's plan completely for your life. Maybe you related to Sheila's, Marie's, or Ann's story. They each made the decision to let go of their preconceived ideas about what it meant to trust God and others. How about you? Are you willing to take a risk in trusting God's plans for your life as the best plans?

Cultivating Confidence in God's Promises

You might be thinking the concept of rebuilding your confidence in trusting others and God is risky and a big ask. I understand. Consider this: if you had to start rebuilding your trust, wouldn't it be less risky to test the waters with someone who has a proven track record of being trustworthy? That someone is God. You can trust him and place complete confidence in what he promises in Scriptures. Numbers 23:19 reminds us about God's integrity and character. "God is not a man, so he does not lie. He is not human, so he does not change his mind. Has he ever spoken and failed to act? Has he ever promised and not carried it through?" You will never be disappointed when you place your complete trust in God.

Here are three powerful strategies to build your trust in God:

Trust in God Strategy #1—Don't lean on your own understanding.

Proverbs 3:5–6 says, "Trust in the LORD with all your heart; do not depend on your own understanding. Seek his will in all you do, and he will show you which path to take." When we become overwhelmed by life our default is to trust in ourselves. We start plotting and planning the strategy of how we're going to get out of this one. The reality is our minds are limited and we don't have the wisdom to solve all our issues. Proverbs 3:5–6 reminds us to simply trust God and his wisdom will lead us to the right solution.

Trust in God Strategy #2—Go to the throne of grace.

"So let us come boldly to the throne of our gracious God. There we will receive his mercy, and we will find grace to help us when we need it most" (Hebrews 4:16). Sometimes we need extra help. We can count on God's help when we need it most or when we hit rock bottom. We can trust God will not abandon us when we are at our lowest point. As we draw close to God, he will draw close to us. When we are struggling to trust God, we can ask God for his grace to help us trust him completely.

Trust in God Strategy #3 – God's character is faithful.

"The faithful love of the Lord never ends! His mercies never cease. Great is his faithfulness; his mercies begin afresh each morning" (Lamentations 3:22–23). In Lamentations 3:18, the prophet Jeremiah confessed his hope was lost. "I cry out, 'My splendor is gone! Everything I had hoped for from the Lord is lost!'" However, in verse 21, Jeremiah says he has hope. Where did he find hope after it was lost? What caused Jeremiah's sudden shift in thinking? His hope returned when he took control of his mind and turned his thoughts in God's direction. He remembered God's faithful love and how his mercies never end. He remembered how God's character is unchanging and how he is a promise keeper. God's faithful love gave him what he needed to trust God again. Jeremiah trusted God's covenant promises over his feelings.

Get Up, Girl, Let's Go Exercise

When someone you depend on disappoints you, how do you typically respond?

The next time you are disappointed, think about a new way you can respond to guard your heart from developing a trust issue.

Imagine God is inviting you to go on a trust walk with him. He is extending his hand toward you and asks you to trust him in writing the next chapter of your story. How would you respond to his invitation?

"Let me hear of your unfailing love each morning, for I am trusting you. Show me where to walk, for I give myself to you" (Psalm 143:8). God wants to remind us we are in a relationship and partnership with him. We can trust him with our lives and future. We can depend upon him to get us through anything. God will give us the wisdom we need to make the right decisions and the courage to stand up for what is right according to his standards, not ours.

Like a little child who trusts in her mom or dad, God wants us to trust him the same way. Children don't plan their future, drive themselves to school, pay bills, buy clothes, or do much related to their care. Their mom or dad does all of that for them without any gentle reminders because parents anticipate the needs of their children in advance because they love them. God's love for us is much deeper than a parents' love for a child. Like a parent, God also anticipates what we need. God created us and has the original blueprint on us. He knows exactly how we are built, what we like, what we don't like, what hurts us, and what makes us smile.

Possibly, there are some things you just can't seem to let go of or give completely to God. Maybe you've been running around in circles having a few temper tantrums because things just haven't gone the way you've thought. Like a parent, God sees further down the road than we do. Maybe God is not allowing you to have something you really want because it's not his best for you. That thing might hurt you, so he snatches it away. The dark road you are going down might be dangerous, so he grabs you tightly by the hand and reminds you not to run away but to stay close. The sweet things you want to taste might make your stomach hurt and stunt your spiritual and physical growth so God says, "No, you can't have that."

Consider the delays and setbacks as indicators God wants you to wait and trust his leading. If you haven't figured out a solution by now it's time to bring in the SME (Subject Matter Expert). A SME knows the intricate details and can develop a strategy to solve a problem because they are the experts in their field. God is a SME when it comes to us. Don't waste any more time trying to figure out your own solutions.

Reflection:

What area(s) do you need to trust God to do the hard work of figuring out what's best for you?

CHAPTER 9

Thinking a New Way

As I mentioned in chapter 5, the average person processes 70,000 thoughts per day. Ladies, what are we thinking about every day? I'm sure I have more thoughts than average because I am an over processor.

Before my feet hit the floor in the morning, I've thought about what happened the night before, mapped out the key points of a conversation I need to have with my children, and created a mental list of the things I need to accomplish in the next sixteen hours. The community in my head starts a conversation reminding me what's not right about my thinking, why I need to second guess a decision, and what a failure I am because I can't juggle ten balls and catch them all simultaneously in one hand.

When I get out of bed there are more things to process—traffic, work projects, ministry items, dinner options, and whether or not I should work out today. I shouldn't be surprised when it's time for my head to hit the pillow and I can't fall asleep. My mind is still processing my day.

Our mind decides what actions we'll take. For example, if we're offered a piece of lemon pie, we first think about whether we should eat it. We might check the label for the fat and carb content and consider if eating the pie has more positive or negative consequences to our digestive system. Possibly, we don't give much thought to the negative aspects of eating the pie. Instead, we decide to just enjoy the various flavors bursting in our mouths with every bite.

Our thoughts shape our personality, emotions, and behavior. If we process a thought long enough it will be birthed in our heart and eventually come out in our actions. Our thinking can be constructive or destructive, or positive or negative. Just imagine how many mistakes started with one thought. God wants us to be mindful of what we are thinking about because our thoughts are powerful and can bring forth life or death to us and others.

Think for a moment about your thoughts. Are most of them positive or negative? Let's look at five positive- and negative-thinking areas. This exercise sets a benchmark to determine whether your thoughts are more negative or positive. Read the positive-thinking focus and then the corresponding negative-thinking focus. On a scale of 0–100 percent, how you would rank your thinking on each line? For example, you might say, "I think of the best-case scenario 70 percent of the time, and the worst-case scenario 30 percent of the time." Do this for each line across.

Positive-Thinking Focus:	Negative-Thinking Focus:
Best-case scenario____%	Worst-case scenario____%
What's right about me and others____%	What's wrong about me and others____%
Future Opportunities____%	Past Failures____%
I see my beauty and uniqueness____%	Other's beauty and uniqueness is greater than mine____%
I am grateful for my life____%	I am dissatisfied with areas of my life____%

Now add the percentages in each column. Check which applies to you:

☐ More positive thoughts____%

☐ More negative thoughts____%

Everyone goes through seasons of processing more negative than positive thoughts. However, we can't stay in a place of negative thinking for an extended time for several reasons:

1. Negative thinking is poisonous. Our mind is our control tower. If we think more negative thoughts, we shouldn't be surprised if our life produces negativity. You can't feed a fruit tree poison and expect it to produce sweet fruit. Think of your negative thoughts as poison trying to kill the best and sweetest parts of who you are.

2. Negative thinking can cause health issues such as colitis, heart issues, migraine headaches, high blood pressure, insomnia, stomach disorders, arthritis, and more. In Psalm 32:3–5, David's

negative thinking grew into the sinful action of committing adultery with Bathsheba. As a result, his strength was drained, and his life was filled with frustration, anger, misery, and achy bones. The consequences of David's negative thinking impacted his emotional and physical health.

3. Negative thinking can give the enemy access to our mind. The devil is clever in setting up strongholds in our mind. A demonic stronghold is defined by Illuminate Community as a demonic fortress of thoughts housing evil spirits that: control, dictate, and influence our attitudes and behavior; oppress and discourage us; and filter and color how we view or react to situations, circumstances, or people.[1] The enemy establishes these mind strongholds through deliberate deception designed to keep us stuck for years. We are deceived when we believe these strongholds are who we are because they have been part of us for as long as we can remember, perhaps even generationally. Examples of strongholds are old, prevailing problems such as a bad habit, a bad attitude, an explosive temper, or a propensity to sin in a certain area. These areas are like cement in our life—difficult and challenging to break through. Later in this chapter we will discuss more about strongholds.

What Feeds Our Negative Thinking?

Consistent negative thoughts about a person or a memory might be God's way of enlightening us, letting us know he wants us to heal at a deeper level. For example, I recently had a conversation with a person who was critical toward me. Within two minutes of being in her presence, she rattled off three negative comments about me. After she was done, and the shock wore off, I asked her, "Is there anything else wrong with me?" She responded, "Why are you getting so defensive?" I left her presence feeling unsafe and wanting to avoid her.

A few days later, after processing our transaction, we had a conversation. I learned her negativity was rooted in my performance not aligning with her beliefs and methods. I told her I felt offended when she judged her thoughts as correct and mine as incorrect. Different is different, not better. I also discovered a deeper meaning to why I was offended. Her comments had triggered a negative memory. This interaction indicated I still harbored a sensitivity to being criticized because of my past. I still needed healing.

Personal biases can also keep us stuck in negative thinking by keeping our mind narrowly focused. Biases are how we subjectively view the world—our experiences, beliefs, values, education, family, friends, peers, and others. Biases are beliefs not founded by facts but instead by our opinions. An example of a bias would be if I think all men are liars, so I avoid them and think they cannot be trusted. However, this statement isn't true of all men. A problem occurs if I allow my bias to guide my perspective about any type of relationship with a man. Because my mind is narrowly focused on my personal negative encounter, I will probably miss out on experiencing some healthy relationships with men, and potentially miss out on meeting my future husband.

Biases can deter us from trying new things. Biases can hinder us from taking risks. And biases can inhibit us from enjoying the beauty of meeting and getting to know others who don't think like us. We can stay stuck by not considering a different perspective, and we must be careful not to let our personal biases lead us into judgmental thinking.

What is a personal bias you have and how has it influenced you to view an experience, person, gender, or group of people negatively?

The Analyze Room

I mentioned earlier I'm an overthinker. Over analyzing can also feed our negative thinking. When we overanalyze, it puts us in the Analyze Room by ourselves where we pick apart and examine every decision in detail. In this room, there is a little community that whispers lies. In this room, thoughts are magnified as bigger and more destructive than they are. In this room, we spend too much time thinking harmful things. We don't see any good. This is the room where the community in our head hangs out and whispers lies about us and others.

In the Analyze Room, thinking becomes dangerous because it floods our soul with anxious and fearful thoughts. This is also the room where Satan trapped Eve. He planted seeds of doubt in her mind about God's goodness, her heavenly identity, and God's plan for her life. Satan would love for us to stay trapped in the Analyze Room for days, months, and years because this is where he can torment us with his lies and accusations.

Declaring War on Stronghold Thinking

As I mentioned earlier, a stronghold is defined as a demonic fortress of thoughts housing evil spirits that control, dictate, and influence our attitudes and behavior; oppress and discourage us; and filter and color how we view or react to situations, circumstances, or people.[2] The word stronghold appears fifty times in the Bible and typically refers to a fortress with difficult access. However, in 2 Corinthians 10:4–6 Paul explains we must declare war against strongholds by using spiritual weapons—not guns, swords, influences, wealth, or being clever. Instead, we use methods that are mighty in God for pulling down and breaking through these strongholds.

The apostle Paul uses the term stronghold to describe our thinking and attitude in 2 Corinthians 10:3–6 (NKJV). "For though we walk in the flesh, we do not war according to the flesh. For the weapons of our warfare *are* not carnal but mighty in God for pulling down strongholds, casting down arguments and every high thing that exalts itself against the knowledge of God, bringing every thought into captivity to the obedience of Christ, and being ready to punish all disobedience when your obedience is fulfilled."

Here are three ways we can declare war on stronghold thinking based on 2 Corinthians 10:3–6:

1. Declare war against negative thinking by bringing every thought into captivity to the obedience of Christ. Bringing our thoughts into captivity means we are:

   - Catching the thought when it comes to your mind, cornering the thought, and inquiring about who sent it. Is this of the devil, or is this of my flesh? Since it's not of God, it does not move past your thinking.
   - Challenge the thought by asking yourself, "Will this thought produce life or death in me?"
   - Coming into agreement with the Word of God about the thought.

2. Declare war against negative thinking by increasing our faith. We establish faith in God's ability by not trusting in our own. In Ephesians 6:16, Paul tells us above all else to put on the shield of faith as a piece of armor to fight the enemy—to extinguish all the flaming arrows of the evil one. Our faith is our protection, it keeps the enemy from getting access to us. We take up the shield of faith by believing what God's Word says instead of what we think. Faith is the certainty of what God says in his Word is true.

3. Declare war against negative thinking by counteracting the negative thought with the truth in Scripture. When Jesus was in the wilderness being tempted by the devil for forty days and forty nights, he used the powerful weapon of repeating Scripture to defeat every manipulative assault the devil used against him.

Renewed Thinking—Winning the Battle by Changing Our Thinking

Scripture gives us some powerful instructions on how we can start and win the battle of negative thinking by changing how we think or renewing our mind. In Romans 12:2, the apostle Paul gives us the solution on how to renew our thinking:

Step 1: Don't love the world by allowing it to squeeze you into its mold. This mold leaves God out. Become a nonconformist like Jesus. Jesus's thinking was only focused on the will of his Father.

Are there any areas of your life where you are squeezing out God?

Step 2: Allow God to transform you into a new person by changing the way you think. You are not doing the transforming, God is. The only thing you are doing is emptying yourself of the things that are squeezing out God. What areas of thinking do you need to empty? What do you need for God to renew in you?

Step 3: When we do steps 1 and 2, God brings our thinking in line with his thinking, and we will discover God's will which is good, pleasing, and perfect.

What Does God Think About?

Did you know God is always thinking about us? He cares for us and has a plan for us. God's plans are not canceled or forgotten when we sin or make a mistake. His love for us never fails. It's important to understand his plans so we have something beautiful and hopeful to think about. Here are some Scriptures about God's beautiful and hopeful thoughts toward us:

- God cares for us: Jeremiah 29:11: "'For I know the plans I have for you,' says the LORD. 'They are plans for good and not for disaster, to give you a future and a hope.'"
- God's thoughts are good and precious toward us: Psalm 139:16–17: "You saw me before I was born. Every day of my life was recorded in your book. Every moment was laid out before a single day had passed. How precious are your thoughts about me, O God? They cannot be numbered!"
- God sees us as valuable: 1 Corinthians 7:23: "God paid a high price for you, so don't be enslaved by the world."

Here are some additional Scriptures to meditate on regarding God's thoughts:

- Psalm 92:5: "O LORD, what great works you do! And how deep are your thoughts."
- Isaiah 55:9: "For just as the heavens are higher than the earth, so my ways are higher than your ways and my thoughts higher than your thoughts."

- Psalm 144:3: "O LORD, what are human beings that you should notice them, mere mortals that you should think about them."

Did you notice a pattern regarding the focus of God's thoughts? God's thoughts are of us. His thoughts are also good, hopeful, detailed, loving, precious, and higher than our thoughts. We are the apple of God's eye.

How Do We Discern If Our Thoughts Are from God?

God's thoughts never contradict Scripture. They are giving, caring, graceful, merciful, full of wisdom, considerate of others, and beyond our normal thinking. God's thoughts are not negative. God began giving me God-thoughts when I was trapped in a pattern of negative thinking about my identity, memories, and my future. Now let me be clear, God wasn't speaking to me audibly. God is a spirit (John 4:24). He spoke first to my spirit and then my spirit translated his thoughts to my mind.

God speaking to me all started when I asked him questions about my everyday thoughts and emotions. His answer came by way of a conversation with me, or he would direct me to a Scripture. Here is a journal entry highlighting one of our conversations:

Daddy,

My faith is low, and I feel discouraged today. Sometimes I feel like I'm not going to make it. I keep getting punched by the enemy through circumstances, and some of them I didn't create. People are messing with me; others want things from me, but I have nothing left to give. My good is perceived by others as evil. If I make a mistake or speak the truth in the most loving way possible, I still get labeled as too strong or too emotional, or it's implied I need to change my personality. I'm sorry if I'm letting you down with my thinking, but I must be honest with you. I just don't have the energy to fight right now, emotionally or spiritually. I'm tired. Life seems so cruel and unfair. I've been in this dry season for way too long. I don't know what I need to do to fix anything; I've tried everything. I've prayed, fasted, stayed encouraged, but the enemy's darts are still coming and hitting me. You said you would not give me more than I can handle. Can't you see I'm at my maximum capacity? Daddy, I need a miracle, a touch from you right now.

God's response:

Daughter,

I know you are weak, and you are struggling to hear and see me clearly in this season, but I'm with you. I know you feel stuck, and your faith is low right now. I'm not trying to break you down—there is not an additional lesson I'm trying to teach you. I'm building you up, so you are prepared for the next chapter of your life. The places I'm planning to take you will require you to be immovable in your faith. I'm teaching you how to cry out to me, seek my face like never before, and encounter me in a deeper way. I desire your faith and trust in me be sustainable whether you are in a fall, winter, spring, or summer season in your life. I don't just want you to know what my Word says, but I want you to encounter me so you will know I'm real.

Although your circumstances look bad right now, I'm working things out for your good. I want you to lean totally on me and to trust me again. I'm not requiring you to figure anything out. Don't worry—

I'm not going to abandon you or leave you alone in this. Trusting me is letting me figure things out for you. I want to remind you that I can hear your faintest prayers. Yes, also the ones when you can only whisper, "Help." I hear your heart, and I see your desperation for circumstances to shift. I just want you to sit back and relax. Let me do the heavy lifting needed in your circumstances. Rest, get your strength back, and hope in me again because where we are going you are going to need it.

These types of conversations with God helped me change my thinking to align with his thoughts about me. God continued to speak to me in this way whenever I asked him a question.

What Does God Want Us to Think About?

God is inviting us out of negative thinking, personal bias thinking, analyze room thinking, and being conformed to the patterns of this world thinking. He is leading us into a new way of thinking: his way of thinking. In Philippians 4, the apostle Paul reminds us where to center our thinking, and the results are a peaceful and positive thought life. We should focus our thinking on:

- Settling Disagreements: We may not agree with another's thinking or methods, but we can agree on what Scripture says. Agreeing about God's Word gives us the freedom to move beyond being right, proving a point, and letting an offense linger.

- Seeking Godly Happiness: The Bible defines godly happiness as joy. Worldly happiness focuses on the circumstantial. If we want to experience the joy of God's promises, Paul encourages us to rejoice whether our circumstances are good or bad.

- Being Gracious: Graciousness involves not spreading negativity and unhappiness to others. Instead, we are to make others feel comfortable and appreciated. God expects us to be welcoming, generous, and forgiving of others quickly. Being gracious helps us respect others and appreciate how they are uniquely different, but still valuable to God. When we see others like God sees them, we won't focus our thinking on areas we feel they need to improve.

- Praying Instead of Worrying: Worry fills our mind with fear. Fear is torment and there is nothing positive about being tormented. Every time worry rears its ugly head, consider it an invitation to start praying. The more we worry, the less we pray and the less we pray the more we worry. God wants us to make our prayer requests with thanksgiving—not for the problem, but for the God who can solve the problem.

Here are some other areas of thinking Paul's tells us to concentrate on:

- True Thinking—not false or unreliable
- Noble Thinking—honorable
- Just Thinking—right toward God and others
- Pure Thinking—moral and good integrity
- Lovely Thinking—admirable and agreeable
- Good Report Thinking—positive outcomes

- Virtuous Thinking—excellent
- Praiseworthy Thinking—deserves to be commended

Get Up, Girl, Let's Go Exercise

Through the revelation of the Holy Spirit, we can start to clearly see the areas where we are stuck in our thinking. Sometimes giving our mind a creative endeavor, such as writing, music, or hobbies can shift us into a new way of thinking. What positive endeavor can you commit to incorporate or expand in your life?

Is there a running negative conversation in your head? Take the thoughts you have been overprocessing and create a new story line with a positive perspective. The Bible says God causes all things to work together for your good. What is the good in your new story?

Empty your mind of thinking negative thoughts for the next ten days. God wants us to move forward in thinking about things that bring possibilities, vision, passion, and purpose in our life.

Reflection:

Spend some time writing down how you desire your thinking to change in the following areas:

Possibility Thinking: List one thing you think is impossible. Write a prayer to God asking him to show you how your thinking can shift into possibility thinking in this area.

Vision Thinking: List three things you are dreaming about for your future.

Passion Thinking: List three things that are important to you and make you smile.

Purpose Thinking: What you are gifted and called to do naturally and spiritually, and how might God want you to use your gifts?

CHAPTER 10

True Confessions of the Heart

Imagine you are holding your heart in your hand. What do you see? If this were possible, you would see the anatomy of your heart—aorta, arteries, ventricles, valves, atriums, and veins. You would be amazed to watch how this less than one-pound organ can pump 2,000 gallons of blood through your body every day as well as regulate many bodily systems.[1] As you know, the heart is one of the most important organs in your body.

Our emotional heart controls our desires, emotions, hopes, and dreams. God gave us a mind and this heart to experience him in two ways. It is with our mind we believe God is who he says he is. With our minds, we intellectually get to know him. However, it is with our heart we trust, experience, and draw close to God in a deeper way.

Are We Taking Our Hearts for Granted?

In my opinion, the needs of our hearts are often neglected. We consistently care for our physical needs—we feed our bodies expensive, organic, and non-GMO food choices, we also make time and financial commitments to exercise to keep our bodies healthy. Our outward person is growing and thriving, but what about our inner person, our heart? Do we understand what is vital for its survival? Why don't we spend as much time and money on our emotional heart health?

What Is Our Heart Saying?

If our heart could speak, what would it say to us? What are its likes and dislikes? What makes it hurt, and what does it need and want? I think if we listen to our heart, it might tell us some deep things. It would probably tell us how it wants to be loved and cared for so it can perform at its maximum capacity. Our heart might also give us the combination to unlock areas where we have been stuck for years. Let's listen to five hearts and hear their true confessions. Journal what your heart might be saying to you about what it needs after each confession.

Heart Confession #1—When You Hurt, I Hurt Too.

I'm so tired of you not listening to me. I keep telling you I'm broken. I've been hurting for years. I ache with feelings of loneliness, despair, and fear. Why do you pretend we are okay when we're not? You've wondered why you keep thinking about your childhood issues, broken relationships, and other disappointments. It's because I'm reminding you. I need your help to heal. I can't do it by myself. Can you please just acknowledge the truth? Say it with me, I hurt.

What's your response to this heart? Have you ignored anything your heart has said to you? Can you commit to listening to your heart?

Heart Confession #2—Love Me, Love Me, Love Me

Do you love us? I'm asking you this question because you continue to allow others to mistreat us. I'm not sure if you understand that true love shouldn't mistreat us or speak ugly words to us. For years, we have taken the higher road, and each time we've taken a hit. Although you say those ugly words don't hurt you, they hurt me because I am part of you. I know they have hurt you too. A section of me has been injured by the ugly words you allow to be spoken over us. I experience ugly words as arrows and darts. You are important to me, and I would like for you not to allow others to take us for granted and mishandle us in the future. Moving forward, will you please start placing healthy boundaries with anyone who insists upon mistreating us with ugly words?

What's your response to this heart? Can you commit to releasing the toxins the ugly words have had on your heart? In the future, what boundary can you put in place not to allow others to mishandle you by speaking ugly words over you?

Heart Confession #3—What Are We Going to Do with All of Our Walls?

You have been afraid you might fail, that you might choose the wrong person to be in a relationship with, or that you might make another financial mistake. You have built walls around me to protect me from future failure and risk, but I'm suffocating and I feel trapped. I want to give you confidence and boldness to break through your walls and install gates, but I hesitate because I see you are comfortable with the solid walls. These walls are limiting us from dreaming, hoping, planning, and feeling loved. I'm being blocked from what I do best, giving and receiving love, which in turn is blocking you from giving and receiving love. Gates will allow you to decide who to let in and have access to us.

What's your response to this heart? Can you commit to tearing down some walls and installing gates to let in only the right kind of love? What is one wall you can reconstruct with a gate?

Heart Confession #4—Stop Attacking Us

Did you know when your inner self-critic speaks negative and discouraging words about you, I can hear everything it says? I take what you say personally. I listened to the conversation you had the other day and

I want to remind you of the words you used, "Never, I am not, I dread, I doubt, I hate, I'm annoyed, I can't, I don't like, and stop it." Your words have become a self-fulling prophecy in your life. I'm confused. Am I supposed to respond to your prayers for hope, strength, and renewal, or to the negative words you say about yourself? I want you to know I respond beautifully to your prayers, but when you start the inner self-critic talk, I get angry with you. I know you are keeping it real, and it's how you feel, but I want you to know your inner self-critic talk is probably canceling your prayers. I'm sure God is confused too. Many external influences are fighting against you, don't join their party.

What's your response to this heart? Can you commit to stop attacking yourself with your own words? What is new, positive inner talk you can say about yourself?

Heart Confession #5—Do You Realize Your Value?

I see how you de-prioritize your needs for the needs of others, but what about your needs? Do you know your needs? Let me tell you what I need—unconditional love, trusting relationships, and reciprocity. I need for you to learn how to guard me. It's not selfish for you to consider what you need and what's best for you. Considering yourself is a way you can love yourself. There are times you have settled for less because you've felt you don't deserve the best. You don't see your true value. But let me tell you something, you are priceless. Please stop selling yourself short, settling for any low bidders who come to devalue you.

What's your response to this heart? What is one change you can implement to make yourself a priority? In what area can you stop settling for less and begin to believe you deserve God's best?

Our Current Heart Condition

Sometimes we can feel our heart's brokenness is beyond repair. There have been times when I have felt like Humpy Dumpty. My heart shattered into a million pieces, and I had no idea how to pick up the pieces and fix them. The thought of trying to pick up the pieces seemed overwhelming.

Understanding our heart's needs and wants is important. A need is what I must have to survive. A want is a desire to be fulfilled. Recognizing our heart's needs and wants helps us better understand our hearts and provides clarity on what is necessary to lead a fulfilling life.

What are five needs of your heart?

What are five wants of your heart?

What injures your heart?

Have you ever wanted to tear out some pages of your life's story, especially the tattered and stained pages? I want to encourage you not to throw away those pages because God can beautifully restore your story by giving you some new, exciting, and beautiful pages. He can use your tattered and stained pages to help others heal and to draw you into a deeper relationship with him. Your life story hasn't ended yet. Be encouraged. God still is writing your restoration chapters.

My heart needed to be healed from a long list of injuries, some I've mentioned in previous chapters. I tried many ways to heal my heart on my own. My efforts included not thinking about what happened, getting counseling, immersing myself in work projects, focusing on a new hobby or new relationship, enrolling in school, and doing other things to keep busy. Being busy was a great distraction but not the best healing solution for my heart. Busyness acted like a blindfold and a shot of anesthesia. I couldn't see or feel the true condition of my heart.

Can you relate to busyness being a great distraction to keep you from seeing and feeling the true condition of your heart? If so, what are the areas of busyness in your life?

My busy efforts to try to mend my broken heart were not sustainable. I would eventually spring a leak and my brokenness would seep through. I decided to do some heart healing work through a ministry focused on healing. I discovered my heart had been damaged from repeated disappointments. I felt like a magnet for disappointments. My heart didn't have a chance to recover from the last disappointment before another disappointment would come and injure it again. Unknowingly, I had carried these disappointments in my heart for years. A drop of water dripping for years on a strong rock will eventually erode the strength of the rock. Disappointments continually attack our hearts like the water attacks the rock. The repeated attacks weaken the heart's ability to heal and work in our lives as God intended.

I searched for a one-time fix-it solution to plug up my brokenness and repair my disappointed heart. Unfortunately, I discovered a one-time fix to heal my heart was unrealistic when it wasn't just one thing that caused the injury. I learned the following as I worked on healing my heart:

- My brokenness had many layers.
- I am not a broken heart specialist, God is.
- I was using the wrong approach to get healed.

I looked within myself to obtain healing, but I didn't have the prescription to heal my heart. God did. I gave God access to work on my heart, and in return, I got a new heart—a heart transplant—with upgraded functionality. God's restoration process for me included two powerful ingredients working together to effectively heal my heart—God's love and grace.

As you can see from the illustrations on the next page, the broken heart can hold our disappointing events. The healed heart has allowed God's love and grace to saturate it and over time the disappointing events start to fade away.

BROKEN HEART

HEALED HEART

My Heart's Healing Journey

God required two things of me as I released the heart healing process to him. First, I needed to be able to discern the difference between the head version of me and the heart version of me, then lead my life from my heart and not my head. Second, I had to protect my heart from future damage.

Requirement #1

I had to get to know the heart version of me and operate in truth and authenticity toward God and others. The head version of me works hard to always be on point, always do the right thing, and to never make a mistake. This is the strong version of me, the side that rarely shows emotions. Her fake and pretentious ways exhaust me.

I'm not sure where I learned not being okay was okay, but I assumed if I showed God and others my true emotions, I would be viewed as weak and lacking faith. The head version of me would go into the fix-it mode if anything started to feel wrong. My need to quickly get back to "okay" damaged my heart more than healed it because I didn't allow my heart to process my disappointments.

God had to teach me expressing my disappointments was perfectly fine. I could admit I was broken, and I could ask him for help. I often recited the Scripture about God being near to the brokenhearted (Psalm 34:18), but I never needed the Scripture to come alive in my life until I felt my heart broken beyond repair. Acting like I was fine and strong hindered God from having complete access to the disappointed parts of my heart. I don't like the head version of me. She stands in the way of getting to know the real me, which is why I broke up with her.

I was introduced to the heart version of myself as I healed from my divorce. I was broken, but in a beautifully broken way. My life started to flow in an easy, uncomplicated rhythm. My five-year plans and goals didn't have the same value to me any longer. God began to change the desires of my heart and drew me into a deeper level of intimacy and authenticity with him. I refer to this new heart version as Tracy 2.0.

Learning to live my life from my heart was God's strategy to completely heal and take me to the next level. I didn't know it at the time, but God was setting me up to be introduced to my life's purpose. If someone had told me God was preparing me to mentor and coach women on how to break free and live free in their lives, I would have smiled, and said, "Really?" Still, there was some additional heart work I needed to do before God would start to fully reveal my purpose, destiny, and his best plans for my life.

During this season, I started to journal. One day the Holy Spirit spoke to me, "Start journaling and what you write will heal your heart."

I responded, "But I'm not a writer."

Even so, I obeyed. I was desperate and willing to do almost anything to heal. God challenged me to get vulnerable and personal with him in my writing. This meant I had to share my heart with him. I knew I needed to do this to get unstuck from a stronghold the enemy tried to trap me in for most of my life—to keep me silent.

As I mentioned in the previous chapter, I would have these conversations with God. I would tell him my feelings, emotions, and disappointments through my writing. I would also find Scripture to apply a God thought to whatever I was processing. My heart started to transform as I immersed myself in reading and applying Scripture. God remained faithful to fulfill his promise of healing me as my journaling recalibrated my heart. I could feel God's healing transformation and renewal taking place in every aspect of my life.

In 2018, my journal writing inspired me to publish a book of devotionals entitled *All Things New! Discovering God's Peace and Protection During Challenging Times.* These heart conversations were the antidote God used to heal my heart.

Requirement #2

I had to protect my heart from future damage. The second approach God used to heal my heart was to teach me how to guard my heart safe from future damage. As God healed my heart, I sought wisdom to avoid potential re-injury.

Because I am a pleaser, I want to make everyone around me happy, but my happiness was rarely taken into consideration. When I didn't communicate my needs and desires, I was perceived as not having an opinion or my opinions were not deemed important. Being viewed as unimportant or being dismissed hurt my heart. Learning how to communicate openly and honestly about my wants and needs challenged me. I learned how to say "No, thank you, that's not what I want or need," or "This is not in my best interest." These types of responses allowed me to establish boundaries and helped others to see me as a human being and not just a human doing.

King Solomon is recognized as the wisest man who ever lived. He said this about our heart: "Guard your heart above all else, for it determines the course of your life. Avoid all perverse talk; stay away from corrupt speech. Look straight ahead, and fix your eyes on what lies before you. Mark out a straight path for your feet; stay on the safe path" (Proverbs 4:23–26).

To guard our heart means to protect it. We are the guard who stands in front of our hearts, watching over everything coming within twenty feet of it. As the guard, we protect our heart from being attacked, poked, and being broken into by thieves. As the guard, we discern the motives of people who seek access to our heart to determine whether they will value, protect, and care for it. If they can honor our heart, they can move past the guard gate. If they don't, access is denied to the kingdom of our heart. Let's explore some other instructions to help us guard our hearts.

Guard What We Say

Solomon tells us to avoid perverse talk and to stay away from corrupt speech. The word corrupt means rotten or unfit for use. Have you encountered people who lie or exaggerate for the silliest reasons? Their motive is to appear to be better than they are. The impact of their corrupt speech and perverse talk is losing credibility.

We are to guard our hearts against people who don't have a filter on what they say. These people believe they are the subject matter experts on everyone's life, and often say hurtful things which damage other people's hearts. The Bible says we are to protect ourselves from people who operate in this manner. We should not allow them past our heart gate because they could wound our hearts.

Guard Against Distractions

Solomon also reminds us to let our eyes look straight ahead. Another way we can keep guard and protect our hearts is by keeping our eyes focused in the right direction. When we focus on God's plans and purpose for our life, not our plans, we're looking in the right direction. Keeping our focus on the will of God will help us avoid distractions which are sure to come. When our hearts get distracted, we can make some emotional decisions we might regret later. Distractions can lead us off course and we can miss out on God's best. Therefore, God wants us to guard where we focus our time and energy.

Distractions come in many ways: relationships, social media, work, hobbies, TV, discouragement, or through our thinking. At times we can get distracted by focusing on a task or detail that is important, but not the most important detail at that moment. For example, in Luke 10:38–42 Jesus visits two sisters, Mary and Martha, at their home. Martha welcomes Jesus and begins to prepare him a meal. However, Mary decides she wants to sit at Jesus's feet and listen to what he is saying.

Martha was busy worrying about what to serve Jesus; she couldn't relax and enjoy this once-in-a-lifetime moment of Jesus being in her home. Martha was frustrated that Mary wasn't helping her and felt her style of serving was better than her sister's. The Scripture says that Martha was distracted by the big dinner she was preparing and approached Jesus to say,

"Lord, doesn't it seem unfair to you that my sister just sits here while I do all the work? Tell her to come and help me."

Jesus's response to Mary was, "My dear Martha, you are worried and upset over all these details. There is only one thing worth being concerned about. Mary has discovered it, and it will not be taken away from her."

Let's guard our hearts against things keeping us overly distracted with details. We must be careful to not allow any distraction to become bigger than our one-on-one time with God.

Guard Where You Go

Solomon also tells us to mark out a straight path for our feet. If we do so, then we will stay on the safe path.

I heard someone say if your mind tells you to go to a questionable place, ask yourself if it would be okay to take Jesus with you. If the answer is no, don't go. When we ponder something, we consider the consequences—this is using wisdom. Wisdom considers what the consequences might be if we say yes or no. Wisdom considers how our decision might impact others today and in the future. It takes time to consider the cost. Wisdom says to pray about the decision and get God's approval first. Wisdom seeks peace and if there is no peace we shouldn't move forward. Wisdom does the best and right thing even when it's hard and uncomfortable. Wisdom overrides the flesh.

In Proverbs 14:12, the Bible says, "There is a path before each person that seems right, but it ends in death." All too often I chose paths that led to heartache, rejection, and years of therapy when I thought they were the right, God-chosen way. I'm sure you would agree with me when I say, I can't waste any more of my life going down roads called "Seems Right Avenue." This path is too risky. The path I want to journey on is called "Sure Boulevard."

Isaiah 33:6 says, "In that day he will be your sure foundation, providing a rich store of salvation, wisdom, and knowledge. The fear of the LORD will be your treasure."

Consider the path you are on. Is it heading in the same direction God is going? Are you experiencing unnecessary emotions because your feet are going in the opposite direction of God's path? Wisdom says follow the path the Lord God is on. His path will always give you peace and rest in your heart.

Guard Putting Things Before God

We must also guard what we value and make as a treasure. Matthew 6:21 says, "Wherever your treasure is, there the desires of your heart will also be." Is your treasure found in material possessions or heavenly things? I've seen how the enemy can try to destroy us by presenting fool's gold as a shiny, beautiful option. If we pursue what looks shiny and appealing to our flesh, we will find no security in these things because they can be destroyed or stolen. What we chase materially only has temporary satisfaction and we will soon discover the meaninglessness of such a chase. The enemy wants us to attach the value of our heart to the things of this world to distract us from pursuing our God-created purpose. But God has designed a purposeful path for us which will bring sustainable fulfillment.

Guard Your Purpose with Wisdom

On the day David sinned with Bathsheba, he decided not to go to war with his army—he abandoned his purpose. He wasn't where he was supposed to be. One day, one distraction, one step in the wrong direction caused David a lifetime of regret.

David let down his guard by allowing his heart to respond emotionally instead of applying wisdom to his reasoning. He didn't consider the cost if he acted on what his mind and heart were desiring and planning. I don't shake my head at David or judge him for making the decisions he made. What I glean from his story is how quickly my heart can deceive me when I allow my emotions to lead the conversation in my head. David's heart came into agreement with his sinful thoughts. David's story also highlights why we must guard our hearts especially when we feel weak and vulnerable.

The Scriptures below convey our heart's potential and God's response. Read each unguarded heart condition and circle the one(s) with which you can identify.

Unguarded Heart/God's Response

Heart Condition	Scripture	God's Response
Evil	Genesis 6:5–6	God was sorry he created man
Perverse (contrary)	Psalm 101:4	God has nothing to do with it
Proud	Psalm 101:5	God will not tolerate it
Trusting our own heart	Proverbs 28:26	God says it is foolish

The heart seeking pleasure	Ecclesiastes 7:4	God says it is foolish
Deceitful heart	Jeremiah 17:9–10	God says it can't be trusted
Out of the heart comes evil thoughts, murder, adultery, sexual immorality, theft	Matthew 15:18–19	God says these things defile a man
A heart who lies to God	Acts 5:3	God says Satan fills our heart to lie
A closed heart— shuts off his heart when someone is in need	1 John 3:17	God's love doesn't abide in him

By contrast, let's look at our heart's potential when we allow God to have total and complete control and access. Read each guarded heart condition and circle the one(s) with which you can identify.

Guarded Heart/God's Response

Heart Condition	Scripture	God's Response
Rejoicing heart	1 Samuel 2:1	God delights and delivers
Teachable heart	Psalm 16:7	God can teach and guide
Wise heart	Ecclesiastes 8:5	God teaches to do the right thing at the right time
Thrilled heart	Song of Songs 5:4	God imparts joy and excitement
A heart that sees God	Jeremiah 24:7	God will reveal himself as your God

A new heart	Ezekiel 36:26	God takes out the stony stubborn heart and gives a tender, responsive heart
A pure heart	Matthew 5:8	God blesses and will see you
A heart that believes and a mouth that confesses Jesus is Lord	Roman 10:9	God will save
A guarded heart	Philippians 4:7	God's peace will come in a way we can never imagine to protect and keep our heart

Get Up, Girl, Let's Go Exercise

List two ways you have left your heart unguarded and two ways you have been guarding your heart.

Create a wise response covenant on how you will guard your heart. Consider helpful boundaries and how your wise heart will overrule your emotional heart in the following areas:

Your Speech:

Your Relationships:

Your Decisions:

Reflection:

For each statement below, create a prayer about how you will invite God to help you guard your heart.

God, I need you to help me guard my heart against hurts by:

God, I need you to help me guard my heart's desires by:

God, I need you to help me guard my heart against becoming hard and prideful by:

CHAPTER 11

Cultivating Friendship with God, Others, and Myself

For some, the word friendship might put a big smile on their faces, but for others, not so much. Our desires for friendships, preferences of who is allowed to be in our friendship circle, and reasons for the friendship can vary based on our positive or negative experiences.

Friendship connections form by personality commonalities, aligned purposes, mutual hobbies, and similar trauma and brokenness experiences. We classify our friendships based on when or where we met the friend. For example, we have childhood friends, high school friends, college friends, work friends, and church friends. Titles are given to friends such as best friend forever (BFF), ride or die friend, girlfriend, boyfriend, and a dear friend.

Friendship is a deeper level of being known by someone and knowing someone else. You know me, and you allow me to be known by you. Friends talk to each other, spend time together, encourage one another, and have fun with each other. Positive friendships bring out the best in each other. However, negative friendships can bring out a side of us we didn't know existed. Harmful friendships could also be significant contributors to why we become stuck in the first place. Mark Twain is rumored to have said, "Keep away from people who try to belittle your ambitions. Small people always do that, but the really great make you feel that you, too, can become great." Oprah Winfrey is credited with the saying, "Surround yourself with those who will lift you higher."

Have any past or present friends belittled your dreams or ambitions? If so, what were their opinions and how did their comments impact you or hinder your progress? Explain. Are you currently still friends with those people?

Have any past or present friends encouraged you to pursue a dream or ambition? If so, what specific things did they do to encourage you? Are you currently still friends with those people?

Discovering Real Friendship Starts with Our Relationship with God

Proverbs 18:24 defines real friendship. "There are 'friends' who destroy each other, but a real friend sticks closer than a brother." This Proverb defines the attributes of genuine friendship in several ways:

1. A man who has friends must himself be friendly— real friendship has reciprocity.

2. It's better to have one true friend than a lot of friends who lead you astray—real friendships lead you closer to God.

3. A friend pretends to be friends, but there are friends who stick closer than a brother. There are fake friends and real friends; real friends are like family.[1]

The friendships we surround ourselves with have a powerful impact on our feelings, desires, and goals. Good friendships have the power to help us heal from loneliness, isolation, and trust issues.

Friendship with God has taught me how to be a better friend to others and myself. Great spiritual and purposeful friendships with others develop when we are also in friendship with God because he is our first friend. When we are in fellowship with God, we can use godly wisdom to select friends and display godly character in how we treat our friends, but without God in the center of our friendships, we can choose the wrong friends, lead friends astray, and potentially wound friends because of selfish motives.

As I have learned to trust God like a friend, I've discovered the importance of vulnerability in our relationship—getting quiet and communicating my heart with him. Being vulnerable with God has encouraged me to be vulnerable in my friendships with others and with myself. Vulnerability helps us not to hide behind our insecurities. It also gives us the courage to set aside any pride, and to show our heart and genuine emotions. If we don't operate in truth in every area of our lives, we present a false and incomplete view of ourselves.

While researching the topic of real friendship with God, others, and myself, I decided to interview a good friend, pastor, and teacher, Dawn Costa, to get her biblical view and perspective on the topic. Pastor Dawn has been the Bible college pastor at Shiloh Church in Oakland, California, since 2011. For years, I have observed and admired how her life has exemplified a genuine friendship with God, others, and herself. Pastor Dawn's responses were insightful, full of wisdom, and challenged me to consider a fresh perspective about real friendships in general. Following are some highlights of our conversation. Join our discussion with your thoughts. Here we go.

Pastor Dawn, how would you define real friendship with God, others, and yourself?

I define real friendship for all three categories with one word—loyalty. I've taken many personality tests, and all have said the same thing—one of my fundamental values is loyalty. I aspire to be loyal in my relationship with God, other friendships, and with myself.

As far as real friendship with God, God calls us his friend because he fully knows us, and he still loves us. What limits us from knowing God as a real friend is we don't fully know him. Real friendship with God means we can be our true selves.

As far as friendship with others, my role as a friend is to encourage and pray for my friends. In addition, I enjoy being a supporting cast friend and cheering them on. If I were to break down what loyalty means to me in friendship with others, it's where I can be honest, my true self. I don't have to hide, wear a mask, or put on a different persona. The deeper the loyalty in my friendships, the more I can be my authentic self. Dawn can show up with my authentic self in many ways—laughter, craziness, silliness, and in spirituality.

Friendship with ourselves means we are accepting of who we are, the things we like and dislike. We must learn to accept things about ourselves and be kind to ourselves. We demonstrate loyalty to ourselves when we are committed to our development, growth, and self-care. Unfortunately, sometimes we are more committed to others' visions and purposes, and we neglect walking in our own.

I agree with Pastor Dawn's response. Friendship with God, others, and ourselves has a common denominator, loyalty. Loyalty means I consistently demonstrate strong support and allegiance in a friendship. I think of loyalty as the glue in a relationship. Without it, a relationship will not stay healthy or be sustainable long-term because loyalty bonds the relationship.

Loyalty in our friendship with God means we are faithful. We demonstrate our faithfulness/loyalty to God when we put him before anything and anybody else. For example, in Matthew 22:37–38, a scribe asked Jesus which of Moses's Ten Commandments was the most important to follow. "Jesus replied, '"You must love the Lord your God with all your heart, all your soul, and all your mind.' This is the first and greatest commandment." What does it mean to love God with all our heart, soul, and mind? This Scripture means we are all in—totally committed and loyal in our relationship with God. God's loyalty for us never ends. In return, we can demonstrate our real friendship and devotion to God by having the same eternal commitment.

Friendship with others is vital to our well-being. God didn't create us to live our lives isolated without community. Being in a community with others satisfies our need to have play in our lives. Play includes laughter and fun. Life is unbalanced when we remain solely focused on work and achievements. As I mentioned earlier, friends can help us move forward into God's best plans for our lives, or they can be a significant contributor for us getting and staying stuck.

God wants us to use wisdom in how we select our friendships. A real, loyal friend is someone who doesn't wound others with their unaddressed areas of brokenness. Instead, they are intentional about being authentic in the friendship, and they have a genuine desire to heal and not hurt a friend.

Friendship with ourselves accepts who we are—the good, bad, and ugly parts of us. We recognize God has fearfully and wonderfully made us unique and special, and we have an appreciation for how God has formed us. When we are our own friend, we do not use others' accomplishments as benchmarks for our lives. Instead, we focus on becoming the God-created best version of ourselves. Being our own friend means we do not feed our souls with judgmental and critical words because we understand God doesn't make any junk. When we criticize ourselves, we are saying to God he made a mistake when he formed us. Being friends with ourselves means we understand what God has for us is for us, and not for anybody else. We don't have to compete, compare, or be jealous of anyone else's mission, vision, purpose, or accomplishments. Our focus is on where God is leading us on our purpose journey. We don't have time to be sidetracked looking at anyone else's journey. Friendship with ourselves also means we do not neglect our emotional, spiritual, and physical needs.

Do you consider yourself one of God's friends? Why or why not? What would it take to help you feel like God's friend?

What are your thoughts about loyalty in friendships? What other characteristics of a friend are important to you?

How are you a good friend to yourself? In what ways are you not being a good friend to yourself?

Pastor Dawn, how has God supported you like a friend?

God has shown up for me as a friend, most recently, in my dating and courtship with my now-husband. I remember getting ready for our first date and asking Jesus to show up as my elder brother. I needed him to coach me. I didn't know how to date, and I also didn't want to make a mistake. I needed the Lord to have my back. I also see God as a friend in my prayer life. One-third of my prayer life is approaching God as a friend in how I communicate with him. Praying to God as a friend has helped me effectively move past religious types of prayers.

I love how Pastor Dawn invites God into her personal life, areas where she is fearful and not as confident— her real places. There have been times when I prayed and asked God if he would approve of a new friend, and if he didn't, to send me a sign. His answer came in a couple of ways. One way was when the relationship simply vanished without cause or explanation. Another sign was my heart hearing God flat out say, "No, do not pursue this friendship." I have learned to honor God's no. Disobeying his no resulted in getting my feelings hurt. I discovered later God was protecting me from what I couldn't see—heartache and rejection.

Friends give each other access beyond a text message or a "like" or a heart on a social media page. In a real friendship, real time is spent with real people. It's also essential for us to give God access to us beyond just a quick prayer. Let's discuss some ways we can provide God quality access to us:

1. Initiate a conversation by asking him questions.
2. Get honest about what's going on in your life— what happened today, what emotions you feel, what help do you need from him?
3. Ask his opinion on a matter.
4. Determine his will by researching Scripture, and then obeying what the Scripture says.
5. Commit to not cheating on God by putting other things ahead of him—no idol worship.

How has God supported you as a friend?

Can you think of any friendships where God told you no, and you later discovered his reason?

Do you have a question(s) for God about a friendship? If so, ask his opinion on the relationship now.

Pastor Dawn, why don't people view God as a friend?

The world has a skewed perception of God because, in my opinion, throughout history he hasn't been presented as the friend to sinners.

The world was able to see God as a friend in the life of Jesus because he is known as a friend to sinners. Jesus is gone, and we now have the Holy Spirit living in us, I believe the world is introduced to God through believers. It is the church's role to introduce God to people as a loving friend.

Pastor Dawn's response is accurate. In some notable instances, God has been presented in a not-user-friendly way. Remember the Crusades. Although those times did not represent a true picture of the nature of God, their impact has lingered. Unfortunately, at times, God has been introduced as judgmental with unrealistic expectations for our lives. Also, he has been seen as a God who expects perfection, expecting us to perform rituals to please him. Who wants to be in a friendship with anyone where the target is unattainable? Not me.

A survey conducted by ABC news stated there are four ways Americans view God:

1. Authoritative

2. Friend

3. Critical

4. Distant

Only 28 percent of the people surveyed viewed God as a friend, but the majority viewed God as judgmental, critical, and disengaged from their life.[2]

The concept of God being unfriendly is also depicted on television, in the news media, in other religions, and in Old Testament Scriptures. Whatever your view might be of God, ask him if your opinion of him aligns accurately with his heart for you. Do you feel God's real character is authoritative, judgmental, or distant?

I'm bothered when people describe me based upon a negative characteristic. If someone says, "She is angry, unforgiving, and selfish," possibly this person experienced me in a bad mood or through another person's point of view. However, those words don't describe me in totality or speak to my heart intentions.

This person does not know the best part of me.

I want to encourage you to set aside any preconceived views you might have about God based upon others' perspectives. Create your own opinion based on the truth of how God presents himself in the Bible. One way we can change our opinions of God is to understand his intentions and motives for us. God's intentions and plans for us are to prosper us, not to harm us. He has plans to give us hope and a bright future (Jeremiah 29:11).

God is the creator of the first friendship between him, Adam, and Eve. We can glean wisdom from their relationship. Genesis 1:26–27 says, "Then God said, 'Let us make human beings in our image, to be like us. They will reign over the fish in the sea, the birds in the sky, the livestock, all the wild animals on the earth, and the small animals that scurry along the ground.' So, God created human beings in his own image. In the image of God, he created them; male and female he created them."

God created us in his image to have dominion and to be like him. God isn't trying to rule over us—he wants us to rule his creation. God is about empowering us to walk in the identity he gave us, not the identity of our circumstances. The creation of man is friendship at its finest. God calls us a friend in John 15:12–15. "This is my commandment: Love each other in the same way I have loved you. There is no greater love than to lay down one's life for one's friends. You are my friends if you do what I command. I no longer call you slaves, because a master doesn't confide in his slaves. Now you are my friends, since I have told you everything the Father told me."

Through our friendship with God, we become more like him. Have you ever known a couple who has been married for years and they start looking alike? It's because of the years they have spent in each other's presence. It's the same with our relationship with God—the more we communicate and spend time with him, the more we start looking and acting like him. He rubs off on us.

What's your view of God?

Has any life event influenced this view of him? Have you been disappointed because you have felt God has not been a friend to you? Explain.

God deeply desires to be our friend and to have fellowship with us daily. Do you also want to be God's friend?

Pastor Dawn, how does our friendship with God help us get unstuck?

Yes, our friendship with God can help us get unstuck. When we begin to understand what Scripture says about God, we get a Holy Spirit perspective, a true view. This truth shifts our mindset to understand more about God's love, purpose, and desire for us. This change is the beginning of freedom and us getting unstuck. A stronghold is a lie we consider accurate. We get stuck when we hold on to this lie and believe it is true. We can get unstuck when we begin to combat the strongholds in our minds with the truth of what God says in Scripture. Deepening our knowledge of Bible Scriptures is key to our freedom. When we begin to see God as a friend, condemnation falls off, and we feel safe. We can then fully take ourselves to God, be open with what we are struggling with, and allow God to minister to those areas of our lives. People stay in their bondage because they don't want to take their stuff to God. God's friendship with us is judgment-free. We are safe with him.

Pastor Dawn provides us with a great solution to getting unstuck—take our stuff to God. The Holy Spirit is our counselor. Talking things out with him brings us a deeper awareness of God's will, and it releases a massive burden off our shoulders. John 8:36 says, "So if the Son sets you free, you are truly free." I like to paraphrase this Scripture and say, who the Son sets free is free for real.

God healed and transformed me as I moved closer to him and allowed him to love me as a good friend. He wanted me to receive his love, peace, and safety. His friendship offered me a judgment-free, guilt-free, and unconditional love path. God didn't place any heavy expectations on me. The only thing required of me was to open my heart and receive his friendship and love.

What is your typical reaction when someone responds to you in a judgmental way?

Do you feel you are judgmental toward your friends, vocally or silently in your mind?

Describe a time when you needed grace instead of judgment?

Pastor Dawn, is there a correlation between faith and friendship?

Yes, Abraham and Moses and other heroes of the faith listed in Hebrews 11 had something in common. They were all authentically themselves with the Lord. They didn't hide from God. We saw their authenticity in their conversation. After Adam sinned, he hid. God doesn't want us to hide. The Lord appreciates people who are honest, just like humans do. I imagine God says, "Be fully who you are, how I created you to be, and we can be good friends." God can trust us if we don't hide. God likes real people!

I was chatting with a friend who is a new Christian. For years, she hid from God because she felt her realness wasn't something he would appreciate. In her mind, she had made too many mistakes and didn't deserve his mercy and grace. She desired to have a relationship with him, but she felt unworthy and didn't know where to start. She felt she had to make herself more presentable first. But after spending some time reading Scripture, she realized God could handle her sin, and she invited him into her heart to take control of her life. She was surprised and delighted to learn she could come to God just as she was, and that was good enough for him.

She also told me when she started to ask for God's grace and help in her life, she noticed how her life began to shift. She made changes in her thoughts and attitude. As she spent more time discovering a friendship with God through real talk, prayer, and reading Scripture, she spent less time worrying and complaining about things she could not control. God's friendship brought her to a new level of peace and satisfaction.

Pastor Dawn, what are the different levels of friendship with others?

There are acquaintances, new budding friendships, friendships in which there is a real connection, and friendships in which you have similarities. There are also friendships in which you don't feel completely safe to be fully known. The highest level of friendship occurs when we can be known and real, rather than being fake or hiding any aspect of life. Also, it's okay to be guarded in your friendships. Jesus had twelve friends, his disciples. He loved them all, but he had a different level of friendship with each disciple. Some he could trust more than others. Some he invited to go with him more, some got to know him more deeply, and three (Peter, James, and his brother John) he invited along to special places like the Mount of Transfiguration, noted in Matthew 17.

I agree with Pastor Dawn's comment. The highest level of friendship is to be known. Put another way, the highest level of friendship is when we can be our most vulnerable and authentic selves. Have you ever had a friend who knew everything about you, but you knew nothing about them? In my friendships, I'm pretty much an open book. However, I had to learn the principle of reciprocity in friendships, which is a mutual exchange of authenticity. If I'm open about my life with a friend, it is not too much to expect my friend to be open with me. If the friendship continues to be one-sided in vulnerability, the friendship will not grow to the highest level. Understanding a friendship will not rise to a higher level of vulnerability is a good thing because this understanding eliminates the frustration and pressure of unrealistic demands on the friendship.

Another way to discern your friendship level is to determine whether the friendship is aligned based on similar values. The Bible tells us not to be unequally yoked. I apply this principle to friendships as well— my friendships must have some alignment in values. I can build a more profound friendship with people who share the same values. What's important to me is my relationship with God. He is number one. If I don't align in the most important areas with a friend, there might be a value struggle in the relationship down the road. When there is a value struggle in a relationship and one-party compromises, the relationship can become controlling.

Pastor Dawn, have you had to let go of any friends?

I have, but only one or two. I don't believe in breaking up with friends. I think you should always be open to reconciliation. I remember a pastor friend told me we should not have any discord with another believer. Discord exists when we may not be mad, but we don't want anything to do with a person. There is tension, but we are also cordial. God's definition of love, mentioned in 1 Corinthians 13, requires us to forgive all things, including the people who have deeply hurt us.

What are your thoughts about Pastor Dawn's comment about not believing in breaking up with a friend?

I've had to let go of a few friendships. It was highly challenging for me to let them go because, like Pastor Dawn, I don't like being at odds or out of fellowship with anyone. I desire to work toward restoration in my relationships. However, sometimes God will bring the separation if you choose to honor God in your friendships. He will remove the people who are not supposed to be in your life, especially if they block or distract you from his purpose for your life. Those friends will fade away. As we grow in our relationship and calling in God, it's wise to assess if our friends are heading in the same direction we are. When a friend can cheer you on your journey, and at times coach you to get to your destination, that can be a beautiful relationship.

Many friendships have dissolved because of unrealistic expectations and unmet needs. The truth is only God can fill the voids in our lives. When we expect a friend to meet a God need, the relationship will become burdensome to the person expected to meet the demand. Placing unrealistic expectations on a relationship is not healthy or sustainable for the friendship and the friend who feels burdened will eventually get angry and resentful, and the relationship will dissolve.

What kinds of expectations should we have of a friend? To answer this question, let's explore what expectations belong to God, ourselves, and our friends:

Expectations for God	Expectations of Me	Expectations of Friends/Others
Emotional healing	Care and guard my emotions	Encouragement
Forgive my sins	Forgive myself because God forgives me	Support and prayer when I need forgiveness
Fill voids in my life	Take my voids to God	Support and prayer when a void in my life needs to be filled
Establish my spiritual identity and purpose	Research Scripture on spiritual identity—not seek the world's way	Guide in the right direction of God's word
Being perfect	Let go of perfection	Display humanity through friendship
Unconditional love—Agape love	Display self-respect and self-love; Love and honor God	Brotherly love

From this chart, did you recognize any areas where your expectations are misaligned?

We can feel rejected when an expectation from a friend is unmet. Consistently examining if our expectation of others is realistic is a wise and healthy practice to guard our hearts and our friends' hearts. Before communicating an expectation, we can ask ourselves, "Who is responsible for meeting this expectation?" We should also ask, "Is my expectation a void belonging to God?"

Try not to hold others to a higher standard than God or yourself. We are happier when we do not have high expectations of others. Having high expectations for what you give, but low expectations of what you expect from others is a mature and safe place to be in friendship with others. Psalm 62:5 (NKJV) says, "My soul, wait silently for God alone, For my expectation is from Him." Having complete expectancy for God alone is the best place to be in friendship with God.

Get Up, Girl, Let's Go Exercise

God will never force us to be in a relationship with him, but he is always pursuing us. We must decide, however, what level of friendship we will have with him. The Bible says if we draw close to God, he will draw near to us (James 4:8). Therefore, if you want a more profound, intimate friendship with God, you need to initiate it.

Describe three ways you can initiate a more profound friendship with God?

Build a plan for healthy friendships in the future. What will you never accept or do negatively in a friendship again? What new criteria will you use to decide your level of friendship with others? Create two additional declarations and find a Scripture for each:

For example:

Declaration #1—I will strive to be in friendships that cultivate the best in me and the other person. "Most important of all, continue to show deep love for each other, for love covers a multitude of sins" (1 Peter 4:8).

Write a letter of forgiveness to someone you need to forgive. Is restoration possible? Is restoration in your heart? Pray about reaching out to this person.

The foundation for every healthy friendship is love. Healthy friendships are motivated by love. In The Passion Translation (TPT) version of the

Bible, 1 Corinthians 13:3-8 is paraphrased for our understanding as follows:

> "And if I were to be so generous as to give away everything I owned to feed the poor, and to offer my body to be burned *as a martyr*, without the pure motive of love, I would gain nothing of value."

As the passage continues, I've added an explanation to each phrase.

> "Love is large and incredibly patient." Friends don't walk away quickly.

> "Love is gentle and consistently kind to all." Friends are kind, not selfish.

> "It refuses to be jealous when blessing comes to someone else." Friends are not jealous.

> "Love does not brag about one's achievements nor inflate its own importance.." Friends are not boastful about themselves.

> "Love does not traffic in shame and disrespect, nor selfishly seek its own honor ." Friends are not prideful or rude.

> "Love is not easily irritated or quick to take offense." Friends are not irritable or angry.

> "Love joyfully celebrates honesty and finds no delight in what is wrong.'" Friends are honest and are not happy when other fails, or injustice happens.

> "Love is a safe place of shelter." Friends are emotionally safe.

"For it never stops believing the best for others." Friends are encouragers.

"Love never takes failure as defeat." Friends endure through every circumstance

"For it never gives up. Love never stops loving." True friendship is never lost.

Reflection:

Based on the love list in 1 Corinthians 13:4–8, think about a friendship in which these love attributes exist. Which characteristics were on display?

Based on the love list in 1 Corinthians 13:4–8, think about an unhealthy friendship in which love was not on display. Which attributes were missing?

Wisdom in moving forward in our friendships is to build them based upon God's definition of love as the foundation.

CHAPTER 12

Path to Purpose

Purpose is an extensive topic. One chapter can't adequately do this life-changing topic justice. The theme of purpose deserves its own book. For this reason, the last chapter here will focus on discovering what God says about our purpose, which I refer to at times as our God-created purpose.

The past eleven chapters have focused on bringing awareness to stuck areas, obstacles, and detours potentially blocking you from achieving your fullest potential in life—your purpose. I want to remind you of some of the transformative work you've done thus far. You have partnered with the Holy Spirit to identify any stuck areas from your past. You have encouraged yourself to open your heart and adopt new confessions to help you stay focused in moving forward. You have discovered how to turn things over to God, embrace your true identity, trust God for your future, and consider new ways of thinking. You have committed to not getting re-stuck by guarding your heart and pursuing good friendships with God, others, and yourself. You have also challenged yourself to go deeper in your relationship with God. You've done some great work ladies, congratulations!

What Is Purpose?

I've asked many people, "Do you know your purpose?" Often, the initial response is a blank stare. Next comes the uncomfortable, confused look, and then the answer, "I'm not sure." During our lifetime, an intrinsic need develops to discover why we were created and if our life has a deeper meaning and purpose. To answer these questions, we must go on a journey to discover our higher purpose, which I call our God-created purpose.

I define a God-created purpose as the original blueprint for what God planned for our lives to be. God created us with a positive purpose in mind. Revelation 4:11 tells us, "You are worthy, O Lord our God, to receive glory and honor and power. For you created all things, and they exist because you created what you pleased."

Likewise, our purpose for ourselves should align with the purpose he has in mind for us. Our good pleasure comes when God is in the center of everything we do in life. We walk in our God-created purpose when we discover our giftings and talents and begin to use them to impact and advance his kingdom. Our God-created purpose brings glory to God. It brings us pleasure and brings God pleasure when we live according to the purpose God has designed.

Sometimes, our mindset toward God is we don't want him to be in the center of our purpose because we don't want him to have too much of an influence in our lives. It's fine for him to have some influence, but not in every area. We say to God, "Thanks for creating me, but I've got it from here. I'm going to spend my life discovering my purpose and good pleasure, I don't necessarily need your help."

The Prodigal Son in Luke 15:11–32 thought he didn't need help discovering his purpose. In this parable, the son leaves his father's house to find the true meaning of his life—his purpose. He asks his father for his inheritance to start his new life, and his father gives him his legacy. Soon after, the son leaves his father's house and wastes his inheritance on extravagant living. He has no money left. The son hits rock bottom. When he comes to himself, he realizes his father's servants are living better than he is. He realizes his best life is at his father's house. The son decides to go back home and ask for his father's forgiveness for his prodigal lifestyle. The parable ends with the father forgiving his son and restoring him into the family.

My favorite part of this parable is the restoration that takes place with the son and the father. Although the son made many mistakes, the father lovingly anticipated his son's return, and embraced him when he did, welcoming him back into the family with unconditional love. This unconditional love is also available to us. God still has a restoration plan and a powerful purpose for us despite our prodigal pursuits and living.

How can you identify with the prodigal son?

Have you searched for your purpose and fulfillment outside of God? If so, explain?

Have you left one purpose to fulfill what you thought was a better purpose? If so, explain.

Do you need to return home to Father God in any areas of your life? If so, explain.

Apart From God, We Can't Discover Our Full God-Created Purpose

Do you feel something is missing in your life? Do you sense you need to accomplish a goal or attain a certain title to be fulfilled and live your best life? Have you been searching for answers on how to satisfy this unfulfilled longing in your life? Possibly, you have considered solutions such as a new adventure, a new move, a new relationship, a new church, or a new job. These solutions are potential ways you can restart your life and find purpose. However, these solutions may not lead you to God's designed purpose for your life. God's plan typically extends beyond our greatest dreams and desires.

God has the original blueprint of our life because he created us. Who better than him to help us discover and pursue the purpose he has planned for us since the day we were formed in our mother's womb? God invites us to come to him to discover the victorious, abundant, and purposeful plans he has for us. Let's bring our questions about any unfulfilled areas of our lives, as well as questions about our future and purpose, to him. Allow him to help us discover the God-created version of ourselves.

Living in our purpose is a guarantee to staying unstuck, walking in freedom, knowing our heavenly identity, and experiencing our best life. In chapter 8, we talked about taking a trust walk with God. I mentioned I had a dream where I was on top of a rocky mountain. I asked Jesus if I would go through another wilderness experience. Jesus took my hand and said, "No, I'm leading you to complete rest and joy." Hand in hand together we leaped across to the other side of the mountain.

Jesus is also extending an invitation for you to go on a trust journey with him. He wants to lead you from an old place to a new and different place. Jesus is leading you away from your stuck areas into your purpose. Please do not refuse this invitation. Your purpose is where your life blooms, where your true identity is discovered and lived out. Your purpose is where you find and use the fantastic superpowers given to you by God. Your purpose is where your spirit stops striving because purpose brings joy and rest. This journey doesn't cost you anything—it's free. However, it will require you to take Jesus's hand and allow him to lead you. Are you willing to let go and respond to his invite when he says, "Let's go"?

Purpose Preparation

If you have been in a dark season, you have been in purpose preparation. God uses our dark seasons to prepare us for the new destination he is leading us into—our purpose. Preparation is needed whenever we move from one place to another. For example, when we move from one house to another, the preparation includes the packing and unpacking process. The packing process is probably the most challenging part of the move because of the hard decisions. What will we keep, and what will we throw away? The packing process uncovers many old things with memories, and we must decide if the old memories have a place in our new house. Will the memory fit into our new decorating scheme, or will it just take up space in the garage?

By contrast, the unpacking process is tedious but fun because the new house represents a new adventure—new purpose, new start, new hope, new people. During the unpacking process, we can put our life in the correct order. The perfect time to clean, dream, plan, reorganize, and recreate should happen before we unpack.

Let's call your new house Purpose, and your old house Stuck. Here are some questions to ask yourself as you move from Stuck to Purpose. I'm giving you my answers as I thought these through.

- Why am I moving from Stuck to Purpose? To get closer to my calling and to make room for better choices.

- What should I leave at Stuck? Fear, rejection, abuse, low-energy, lack of courage, and anything not motivating me to dream.

- Where is Purpose? A deep place in my soul.

- What are the main streets to get to Purpose? Stillness Avenue and Quiet Rest Place.

- Describe Purpose? A beautiful place where my God-given superpower gifts and talents are on display.

- What should I take to Purpose? Peace, creativity, persistence, courage, commitment, and belief in myself.

- How should I decorate Purpose? With all things to uplift my soul, make me smile, laugh, and draw closer to God.

How would you answer the above questions about your move to Purpose?

1. Where is Purpose?

2. What are the main streets to get to Purpose?

3. Describe Purpose.

4. What should I take to Purpose?

5. How should I decorate Purpose?

What memories of your old life will you leave behind at Stuck?

For years, I've been on a journey to discover my purpose. When I first started this journey, I had a sense of urgency to discover it ASAP. I felt I had wasted many years of being non-purposeful and desired to make up for the time I wasted. God still had some amazing plans for me. I thought I had wasted time, but I discovered I hadn't wasted any. I was right on schedule for God to begin revealing my purpose in a different way than I imagined. Here is what I learned on the journey to discover my purpose.

1. Purpose is a process, not a destination.
2. Purpose—It's not about me.
3. Purpose comes alive through our deepest pain.
4. Purpose comes looking for you.
5. Purpose is now not later.

Purpose Is a Process, Not a Destination

My grandmother, Leora Mae Overall, lived until she was ninety-seven years old. She is my shero and an example of a woman who walked out her purpose until the day she went home to be with Jesus. From childhood, I observed two areas of her life where her purpose was personified. The first area was how she served and loved God. She consistently pursued ways to deepen her spiritual walk—her fire for God never went out. Two weeks before she passed away, she was still talking to God about her purpose. In her rocking chair, gliding back and forth, she asked him, "What would you have me do now?" She was ready for her next God-assignment even at ninety-seven years of age.

Although family members did not fully understand some of things my grandmother would say as she prayed, we figured God was speaking back to her. She would listen and then respond surprisingly with comments like, "My seed? What else is in the books?" Possibly, God was giving her a rundown of all the pages of her life—how she had won souls for the kingdom, and how she had lived a life of purpose doing his will.

The second area of purpose evident in my grandmother's life was how she passed her love for

God down to her family. Although life served her some painful and challenging circumstances, she pushed through them on her knees. She had six children, became a widow at age forty, and was a present grandmother to her forty-eight grand and great-grandchildren. I appreciate the spiritual legacy my grandmother has passed down to the third generation in our family.

My grandmother taught me two things about purpose. First, purpose aligns with your passions. Second, purpose is evident in what you value most. She loved and was passionate about God and her family. Her final words to our family were, "Be sweet and carry on." Her purpose statement was for us to carry on with her legacy of loving God, family, and others. This was Leora's great commission.

Purpose—It's Not About Me

Rick Warren's book *The Purpose Driven Life* has sold over fifty million copies since it was published in 2002. This book is the most translated book short of the Bible—being translated into 137 languages. Recently, I watched an interview with Rick Warren, and he said he had no idea how he would be tested by writing "It's not about you" as the first four words of his book. However, for the past twenty years, he has been tested, sometimes fifty times a day, with the words "It's not about you." If he hears a compliment, he is reminded, "It's not about you, Rick." If he hears criticism, he's reminded "It's not about you, Rick." Sometimes, he wishes he hadn't put those four words in the book because of the implications he has had to personally live out.[1] But those first words of *The Purpose Driven*

Life still ring true—it's not about us. Our lives are about God and his purpose for us.

Rick Warren wrote *The Purpose Driven Life* because, as a pastor, he witnessed people on their death beds finally realizing what mattered most. He is quoted as saying, "When people were dying, they wanted people around them, not their money, trophies, or houses. They wanted love."[2] Warren wrote the book to inspire people to receive God's love, and to love God back—this is our most important purpose in life.

In Ecclesiastes 1:12–2:26, King Solomon is expressing his quest to discover the meaning and purpose of life. He set out to find the true meaning of life and wanted to find the good life. As a wise and wealthy man, he knew if anyone could find the meaning of life, he could. He went on his purpose journey, but without God. As he traveled his journey, King Solomon observed several things:

> "I, the Teacher, was king of Israel, and I lived in Jerusalem. I devoted myself to search for understanding and to explore by wisdom everything being done under heaven. I soon discovered that God has dealt a tragic existence to the human race. I observed everything going on under the sun, and really, it is all meaningless—like chasing the wind." (Ecclesiastes 1:12–14)

Solomon concluded everything in life was futile like smoke. You can't grab smoke, there is nothing to hold on to, it just blows. He couldn't find fulfillment or lasting satisfaction despite his titles, education, and wealth. Solomon failed to discover his purpose—the true meaning for life—because he searched for it in the wrong places. In Ecclesiastes 12:13, he resolved, "That's the whole story. Here now is my final conclusion: Fear God and obey his commands, for this is everyone's duty."

Bottom line, everything in this world could not satisfy Solomon's heart. He believed in God, but his life ended with regrets. Solomon's idol worship and many women distracted him from discovering the true meaning of life—a loving and satisfying relationship with God and a life without regrets.

Purpose Comes Alive Through Our Deepest Pain

Sometimes, God prepares us for our purpose through a process called pain. Pain is a great teacher. Think for a minute about what you have been through in your life. Good news, everything you have been through, God can use for a good purpose. God doesn't waste our pain in any way. Pain teaches excellent lessons, increases our wisdom, gives us courage to establish boundaries, allows us the freedom to say no thanks, and qualifies us to serve, minister, encourage, teach, preach, and evangelize others. Pain can create a beautiful testimony in us that has the power to transform others.

I'll never forget when I told my counselor I wanted the pain I felt to go away.

"Why? Pain is a gift from God?" she said.

I countered, "How is pain a gift?"

She answered my question, but I honestly can't remember what she said. I wasn't listening to her response. Instead, I began to process how God would turn the ugliness of my life into something good. Romans 8:28 says God causes everything to work together for good for those who love him and are the called according to his purpose, but I didn't comprehend that *all* things included my pain. Years later, I understood how God was positioning me to discover my purpose through my pain. Here is what happened:

- My pain drew me closer to God.
- My pain started opening doors for me to minister to other women who had a similar pain story.
- My pain encouraged me to start a divorce recovery group.
- My pain gave me a greater compassion for others.

Sometimes God uses the pain of our lives to get our attention and to push us into our purpose. Through my pain, I discovered my purpose—mentoring and coaching women to go deeper in their walk with God.

How can your pain play a part in your purpose?

Consider how God might want to use your pain to launch you into your purpose. What good do you see, and how might God be positioning your purpose?

Purpose Comes Looking for You

Our purpose will find us. I experienced this when open doors, divine setups, and new assignments I didn't raise my hand for came knocking on my door.

One day the women's pastor at my church asked me to be part of her leadership team.

I told her, "I'm not equipped or ready for this role because I'm still healing."

She said, "You would be perfect to minister to other women who are healing too."

A few months later, the mentoring director at my church approached me and said, "I need someone to take over the individual mentoring ministry, and God highlighted you as the person who would be perfect."

Again, my response was, "I'm still healing."

She smiled and said, "God told me you were the person."

How do you say no to God? Purpose introduced me to my spiritual calling when I least expected it and when I didn't feel ready or qualified.

Purpose Is Now, Not Later

Our purpose might be staring us right in the face. We can miss a purpose door God might be opening for us, however, because we feel we're not ready, or if we're looking into the future instead of focusing on the present.

During a season of tremendous emotional pain, a friend of mine started to collect and care for orchids. She noticed the time she spent caring for her beautiful plants brought her peace and healing. She called this her orchid therapy time. Now, she wants to start a ministry in which she teaches people how to heal through Bible study and caring for orchids. The mission of her ministry is to help hurting people refocus their attention on caring for another living thing. Caring for the orchid will eventually lead to also desiring self-care and seeing new beauty and purpose in their lives. My friend discovered her purpose out of her pain, and through what she was passionate about—God and orchids.

Jesus, a Man with Extraordinary Purpose

Jesus didn't struggle with finding his purpose. He walked in his purpose in everything he did. His purpose was clear—to do the will of his Father. His purpose was to restore sinners to God, so they would have eternal life and live with God forever. His Father gave him his purpose—he didn't have to discover it. Jesus's purpose was fulfilled because he remained obedient to the will of his Father. John 5:19 states, "I tell you the truth, the Son can do nothing by himself. He does what he sees the Father doing. Whatever the Father does, the Son also does."

Jesus didn't act according to his own will. He and the Father were one in their purpose. Let's look at aspects of Jesus's life and notice how everything he did pointed to his purpose.

Satan knew Jesus's purpose was huge and would benefit others. He did not want Jesus to fulfill his Father's will. Satan's attacks started when Jesus was only a toddler. When Herod heard the news about the birth of the Messiah, he ordered the execution of all male children two years old and younger. This was Satan's first attempt to destroy Jesus's purpose. Mary and Joseph fled to Egypt to avoid Herod's diabolical destructive plan.

Mary and Joseph couldn't see the whole purpose of their son Jesus's life yet, but they moved forward in God's will. They were purposed to be Jesus's parents because God knew they would listen to instructions, and he could count on them to obey his will.

Sometimes we must also flee situations such as evil people, jobs, or relationships. The enemy's goal is to get us off our purpose journey. He wants to destroy the purpose seeds we are carrying too.

Creating Your Spiritual Purpose Legacy

I believe as we allow God's love to transform us, our purpose for relationships, personal life, career, and ministry will be discovered and evolve from our connection with God. Our life represents the same illustration mentioned previously about Jesus's ministry pointing back to his Father's will. Jesus's ministry is an example that shows us how we should also live a purpose-filled life—everything we do ought to point to God.

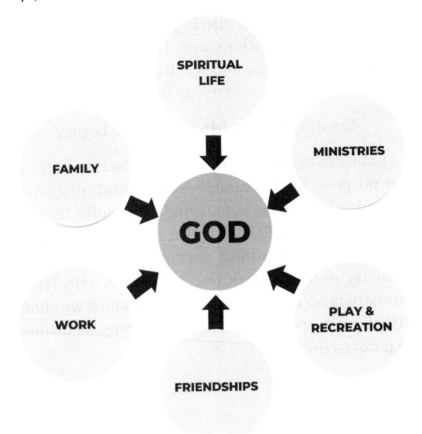

Where Do We Start in Discovering Our Purpose?

When someone is dying or leaving us, their last words become significant. In Matthew 28:18–20, Jesus leaves his disciples with some powerful last words known as The Great Commission. These words also answer the two questions presented earlier in this chapter—why were we created and does our life have a deeper meaning? Here is what Jesus told his disciples about why they were created and how their lives would get better. There was more for them than what they had already witnessed.

"Jesus came and told his disciples, 'I have been given all authority in heaven and on earth. Therefore, go and make disciples of all the nations, baptizing them in the name of the Father and the Son and the Holy Spirit. Teach these new disciples to obey all the commands I have given you. And be sure of this: I am with you always, even to the end of the age.'"

Jesus's last words to his disciples contained their instructions to guide them from their present purpose into their next. Here are the three things they were commissioned to accomplish in their new purpose:

1. Go and make disciples everywhere.
2. Baptize others in the name of the Father and the Son and the Holy Spirit.
3. Teach new disciples—instruct others on how to love God and go deeper in their relationship with him.

For years, Jesus had been a great mentor to his disciples, and now it was time for them to put into action what they had learned from him and seen him do. Jesus starts his commission by reminding them all authority in heaven and on earth has been given to him by his Father. He is now passing the authority baton to continue the work he started. Jesus ends by reminding them he will always be with them if they obey his instructions. Jesus would help them walk into their purpose. They didn't have to figure it out by themselves.

This passage of Scripture is also our commission and guidance to help us understand our next level—our new purpose. Jesus is also with us to help us as we take one step at a time. Remember, purpose is a process, not a destination. I refer to The Great Commission as my "Go." This is my God-created purpose which is connected to God's will. What is God's will? For us to advance his kingdom, like the disciples.

When we become Christians, the Holy Spirit gives us one or more spiritual gifts. These special superpower abilities help us fulfill the Great Commission. In the following Scriptures, the apostles Paul and Peter encourage us to not be ignorant of these gifts and the reasons for them.

"Now, dear brothers and sisters, regarding your question about the special abilities the Spirit gives us. I don't want you to misunderstand this" (1 Corinthians 12:1).

"God has given each of you a gift from his great variety of spiritual gifts. Use them well to serve one another" (1 Peter 4:10).

"A spiritual gift is given to each of us so we can help each other" (1 Corinthians 12:7).

It's our job to understand our gifts. These gifts help us fulfill The Great Commission and help us understand God's best plans for our personal lives.

What are these gifts? You can find the core gifts in Romans 12:6–8, 1 Corinthians 12:8–10, and Ephesians 4:11, 1 Peter 4:9. This list is not all inclusive.[3]

1. Prophecy
2. Service
3. Teaching
4. Exhortation
5. Giving
6. Leadership
7. Mercy
8. Wisdom

9. Knowledge

10. Faith

11. Healing

12. Miracles

13. Discerning of Spirits

14. Tongues

15. Interpretation of tongues

16. Apostle

17. Helps

18. Administration

19. Evangelist

20. Pastor

21. Hospitality

Here are some suggested steps on how to discover your gift(s):

1. Research what the Bible says about your purpose.

2. Listen to what God is saying to you and obey.

3. Take a spiritual gifts test to understand where you might be gifted spiritually. I recommend www.spiritualgiftstest.com. There is also an accompanying book/guide written by C. Peter Wagner called *Discovering Your Spiritual Gifts.*

4. Share and discuss your spiritual gift test results with your pastor or friends and ask for their feedback.

5. Start volunteering at your church or local community in areas where you are gifted.

6. Surround yourself with a community of people who are also discovering their spiritual purpose. We often learn and grow in our purpose together.

7. Allow God to lead you in every step of your purpose walk.

Matthew 6:33 gives us some great advice on where we are to keep our focus as we continue our purpose journey. "Seek the Kingdom of God above all else, and live righteously, and he will give you everything you need." Everything we need includes peace, joy, fulfillment, answers to why we were created, and a guide for our lives to stay unstuck.

Get Up, Girl, Let's Go Exercise:

You started this book mapping out ten important past events. Consider if any of these events could be a new path God might use for you to discover your purpose. What are your thoughts?

List five events you would like to be part of your future. Then, ask God if they are part of his will for your life. What can you commit to doing to find out?

How will you stay on your God-created path to your purpose? Creating a spiritual plan is one way. What spiritual goals can you include in your plan?

Which of your gifts will help you fulfill The Great Commission? Which ones might you be using currently?

A Get Up, Girl, Let's Go woman lives her life with no regrets. Her life exemplifies "She Did It." She is a woman who has been through the fire but doesn't look or smell like smoke. The fire has refined her and made her more beautiful inside and out. The refining fire has transformed her into a pure diamond. She has greater clarity because the fire has burned away distractions and now she sees the truth about her precious value. The fire has taught her to never settle or compromise for less than her value. Although life circumstances happened and continue to happen in her life to get and keep her stuck, she doesn't stay stuck for an extended period.

The fire uses a higher standard to define her, not based upon her outward appearance, but upon the beauty of her heart. She loves the skin she is in, including her flaws. Her flaws tell a redemptive story about her life—they have made her into the fearfully and the wonderfully made unique woman she is today. The refiner has kept her in the fire long enough to bring out her kingdom value, her highest potential, her purpose. She has learned to listen to the refiner's voice. He alone gives her the strength to press forward. He is cheering her on, saying, "My girl, you can do it. My girl, you will make it. My girl, stay the course. My girl, it's going to get better, and my girl, I am with you."

She realizes going back to the old way of living is not an option. Her past is no longer a safe place where she is comfortable. The refining process has empowered her to break free from any and everything holding her captive and in bondage. She breaks down thick walls, kicks boulders out of her way, and hurdles over high things intended to keep her caged. She moves forward with strength. Her inner strength comes from her God, her friend who cheers her on to keep moving forward because he has a beautiful plan on the other side of her pain. He wants her pain to become the motivation to propel her into her purpose. She might be moving at a slow pace now, but soon she will be walking, skipping, leaping, and eventually running in her purpose. Despite everything, she keeps moving forward because no matter what, she must achieve her destiny. A Get Up, Girl, Let's Go woman walks in her God-created purpose one step at a time, leaning on her beloved God the entire journey.

Reflection:

Read the Scripture below and answer the questions:

> "Show me the right path, O LORD; point out the road for me to follow. Lead me by your truth and teach me, for you are the God who saves me. All day long I put my hope in you" (Psalm 25:4–5).

My right path is:

The road the Lord wants me the follow is:

The truth and lessons God is showing me are:

God is saving me from:

My hope is in God for these areas in my life:

ABOUT THE AUTHOR

TRACY LORRAINE HESTER is a Christian life coach, speaker, and Bible teacher. A graduate of Northern California Bible College, she received her BA in Biblical Studies. Tracy is the founder of Women of Purpose, a ministry that focuses on the restoration and healing of women. She is also the cofounder of Reign! Speaking Life & Truth, a weekly podcast that features women's issues.

Tracy is the mentoring director at her church. She is passionate about empowering women whose life issues have wounded them. In 2019, Tracy started a mentoring group called Kingdom Women. The group's goal is to discover their true identity based upon God's Word and move past any negative identity and patterns that keep them stuck in fulfilling their God-created purpose. Tracy lives in Hercules, California, and has two children and a new grandson. Check out her website at tracyhester.com.

END NOTES

Chapter 1–Unlocking Where the Stuck Started

1. Ashley Strickland, "Preserving the Unique History of the La Brea Tar Pits," CNN.com, October 11, 2019, https://www.cnn.com/2019/10/11/world/la-brea-tar-pits-3d-scanning-scn/index.html.

2. "What Are the Tarpits?" La Brea Tar Pits & Museum, n.d., https://tarpits.org/experience-tar-pits/la-brea-tar-pits-and-hancock-park.

3. Vanessa Van Edwards, "The 5 Relationship Patterns: Which One Are You?" Science of People, November 9, 2018, https://www.scienceofpeople.com/relationship-patterns/.

4. John Townsend, *Hiding from Love: How to Change the Withdrawal Patterns That Isolate and Imprison You* (Grand Rapids: Zondervan Publishing House, 1996), Back cover.

Chapter 2–Creating Your Life Map

1. Sharon Stokes, "Benefits of Creating Your Life Map," Sharon Stokes, August 29, 2016, https://sharonstokes.ca/benefits-of-creating-your-life-map/.

Chapter 3–Facing Your Past

1. Nancy Leigh DeMoss, *Lies Women Believe: And the Truth that Sets Them Free*, (Chicago: Moody Publishers, 2007), 215, 218, 236.

Chapter 4–Surrendering Your Broken Parts

1. *Oxford Lexico.com English Dictionary*, Oxford Lexicon, s.v. "surrender," accessed August 4, 2021, https://www.lexico.com/en/definition/surrender.

2. *Merriam-Webster.com Dictionary*, s.v. "surrender," accessed August 4, 2021, https://www.merriam-webster.com/dictionary/surrender.

Chapter 5–Negative Thoughts and Emotions

1. Jon Westenberg, "You Have 70,000 Thoughts Every Single Day—Don't Waste 'Em," *Observer* (blog), May 9, 2017, https://observer.com/2017/05/you-have-70000-thoughts-every-single-day-dont-waste-them-decision-making-process/.

2. Tim Scott and Beth Scott, *Stand and Deliver*, (Maitland, FL: Xulon Press, 2004), 120.

3. "The Tree of Unwanted Behaviors," Hope in Life Ministries (handout), a division of Elijah House Ministries 1989. Used with Permission.

Chapter 6–Turning It All Over to God

1. "How Do I Accept Christ?" The Church Without Walls, accessed August 4, 2021, https://churchwithoutwalls.org/accept-christ/.

2. Mary Fairchild, "Rededication Instructions and Prayer," Learn Religions, updated April 10, 2019, https://www.learnreligions.com/prayer-of-rededication-700940.

3. David Brenner, *Surrender to Love, Discovering the Heart of Christian Spirituality*, (Downers Grove, IL: InterVarsity Press, 2015), 32.

Chapter 7–Discovering Your True Identity

1. "Mirror, Mirror: A Summary of Research Findings on Body Image," Social Issues Research Centre, SIRC.org, accessed August 4, 2021, http://www.sirc.org/publik/mirror.html.

2. "We Spend a Shocking Amount on Beauty Products," Yahoo! News, June 23, 2017, https://www.yahoo.com/news/spend-shocking-amount-beauty-products-174300232.html.

3. "Vanity Costs American Women Nearly a Quarter of a Million Dollars," New York Post, July 6, 2017, https://nypost.com/2017/07/06/vanity-costs-american-women-nearly-a-quarter-of-a-million-dollars/.

4. *Merriam-Webster Online*, s.v. "identity," accessed August 5, 2021, https://www.merriam-webster.com/dictionary/identity.

5. Yourdictionary.com, "Identity Meaning," accessed August 5, 2021, https://www.yourdictionary.com/identity.

Chapter 9–Thinking a New Way

1. "Notes on Strongholds," Illuminate Community Church, 2019, https://illuminatecommunity.com/wp-content/uploads/2019/10/Week-5-Additional_Notes_on_Strongholds.pdf.

2. Tim Scott and Beth Scott, *Stand and Deliver*, (Maitland, FL: Xulon Press, 2004), 120.

Chapter 10–True Confession of the Heart

1. "Habits of the Heart, Lesson 2: Keeps on Pumpin'," Science Museum of Minnesota, accessed August 4, 2021, https://www.smm.org/heart/lessons/lesson2.htm.

Chapter 11–Cultivating Friendship with God, Others, and Myself

1. William McDonald, *Believer's Bible Commentary*, (Nashville: Thomas Nelson, 1990), 839.

2. "A Look at the 4 Ways Americans View God," ABC news, October 7, 2010, https://abcnews.go.com/WN/book-religion-examines-ways-americans-perceive-god/story?id=11825319.

Chapter 12–Path to Purpose

1. "Rick Warren (the Purpose Driven Life): Understand & Accept God's Love: FULL EPISODE: Praise on TBN," YouTube, May 19, 2021, https://youtu.be/ZneXln1UtS8.

2. Ibid.

3. C. Peter Wagner, *Discover Your Spiritual Gifts*, (Bloomington, MN: Chosen Books, 2015), 25–28.

Made in the USA
Monee, IL
24 April 2023